Contents

Getting started

Before you can use the Internet, you need to get connected to it. This chapter explains what that means and outlines your options. It also shows you how to set up a new connection and run Internet software.

Covers

Chapter One

Introduction to the Internet

The Internet is a 'network of networks' that connects computers from all around the world. It's estimated that over 500 million people use the Internet, and the number increases every day.

You can use the Internet to access the latest news; research almost any topic you can imagine; shop for products and services; and get information about your favourite sport or pastime. You can also send messages to your friends, participate in discussion groups and obtain software for your computer.

History of the Internet

The Internet has its roots in 1969, when the US Government decided to connect up some of its computers so scientists and military agencies could communicate more easily. The system had to be very robust, so there was no control centre. Each machine operated independently and messages travelled by any convenient route. Even if some computers were destroyed by a military or terrorist attack, the others could carry on exchanging information.

In the 1970s several more computer networks were established by military and academic institutions. Eventually many of these networks were linked together, creating the network of networks we now know as 'the Internet'. During the 1980s the Internet was dominated by scientists, academics, computer experts and students, but the user-friendly software of the 1990s encouraged a much wider range of people to make use of it.

Although some parts of the world are better represented than others, the Internet is a global phenomenon. You can connect to a computer in Australia or New Zealand as easily – and as cheaply – as to one just down the road.

No-one owns or controls the Internet, although there are several organisations that try to keep everything running smoothly. It can be creaky, cranky and intensely irritating, but for the most part it works remarkably well.

The World Wide Web

The recent surge of interest in the Internet is due to the World Wide Web. Developed in 1990 at CERN, the European Laboratory for Particle Physics, the Web consists of millions of magazine-style pages. Unlike pages in a printed magazine, however, they can

The World Wide Web is not the same thing as the Internet. The Internet is a network of computers. The Web is a service that uses the Internet to transfer information from one place to another. Other services include e-mail (Chapter 8) and newsgroups (Chapter 9).

include sound samples, animations, video clips and interactive elements as well as text and pictures.

Web pages are connected together by 'hypertext' links – electronic cross references that enable you to jump from page to page by clicking on underlined text or highlighted images. A page stored on a computer in London might have links to pages stored in Moscow, Tokyo and Washington, which in turn might be linked to pages in many other countries. The result is a network of connections stretching right around the globe – hence 'World Wide Web'.

You don't need to know where any of the pages are, because you can follow the links. However, if you know the address of the page you want to view, you can jump straight to it.

Turn to Chapter 5 for more information about some of the most popular pages on the Web.

Anyone can create a Web page, so there's a huge range of material to explore. Government departments, museums and educational institutions are pouring information on to the Web, and companies use it to promote their products or sell directly to the public. Publishers and broadcasters produce on-line magazines and news services, and there are many personal Web pages dedicated to the hobbies and interests of private individuals.

Electronic mail and instant messaging

If the Web is the Internet's pretty face, electronic mail ('e-mail') is its useful right hand. E-mail enables you to send messages to other Internet users, quickly and cheaply. It's a great way to stay in touch with friends and relatives, and very useful in the business world.

Instant messaging is an alternative to e-mail. It enables you to hold 'live' conversations over the Internet, either by typing comments back and forth or by speaking into a microphone.

Internet software

You need special software to look at (or 'browse') Web pages, send e-mail and transmit instant messages. Windows XP includes programs for all three activities.

Activity	Program	Covered in
Web browsing	Internet Explorer	Chapters 1 to 7
E-mail	Outlook Express	Chapters 8 and 9
Instant messaging	Windows Messenger	Chapter 10

Connecting to the Internet

Before you can access the Web or send e-mail, you need to be connected to the Internet. There are four possibilities: your company or university may provide a direct connection; you can visit a cyber café or public library; you can use a modem (a device that enables computers to communicate over a telephone line) to connect your home computer to the Internet; or you can sign up for a high-speed 'broadband' connection.

Company connections

The rest of this chapter assumes you're using a modem to connect to the Internet. If you're accessing it via a company network, a cyber café or a broadband service, someone will set up the connection for you.

If you are at university, or work for a large company that has an internal computer network, you may already be connected to the Internet. The advantage of a company connection is that you don't have to pay for it. However, you have to be at work to access the Internet and there may be rules about what you can use it for.

Cyber cafés, pubs and libraries

The cyber café is the Internet equivalent of the public telephone, although it's generally warmer and more comfortable. You can drink coffee (or beer, in a cyber pub) and use the café's computers to access the Internet. Most charge by the half hour or hour and the rates are quite reasonable. Your local library may also have computers you can use.

If you aren't sure whether the Internet is for you, paying to use someone else's equipment for a few hours is a good way to find out. You don't have to worry about setting up the software and there's usually someone to help with any problems. However, you may not have access to the full range of Internet services – for example, you may not be able to send and receive e-mail.

Dial-up connections

The most versatile option is to use a modem to connect your home computer to the Internet. Regrettably, this is also the option that requires the most input – both financial and technical – from you.

You need five things to establish a dial-up connection:

1   A computer. You can connect to the Internet using most types of computer, but this book deals specifically with PCs running Windows XP. If you have an older version of Windows and want to upgrade to Windows XP Home

Edition, check that your PC has a processor speed of at least 233MHz (300MHz recommended), 64Mb of RAM (128Mb recommended), upwards of 1.5Gb of free space on the hard disk, and a Super VGA (800x600) graphics card and monitor. A more powerful computer with more RAM and a bigger hard disk will make using the Internet more enjoyable.

V.90 modems don't actually run at 56kbps – that's their theoretical top speed. In reality, they operate at 45–50kbps.

2   A modem. Most new computers have an internal modem. If you need to buy a modem, an external model that connects to one of the sockets on the back of your PC is easier to install. Make sure it conforms to the V.90 standard, giving it a top speed of 56kbps (kilobits per second).

3   A telephone line. You'll be making a phone call, usually at the local rate, each time you connect.

4   An Internet service provider, or ISP (see overleaf). A service provider has a computer system that is permanently connected to the Internet, and to a bank of modems. You use your modem to connect to one of your service provider's modems, via your telephone line, thereby making your computer (temporarily) part of the Internet.

5   Internet software. Windows XP includes everything you need to get connected and start using the Internet.

Broadband connections

The technology used to provide high-speed connections over a regular telephone line is called 'Asymmetric Digital Subscriber Line' or 'ADSL'.

If you intend to use the Internet a lot, you may want a faster connection that doesn't tie up your phone line. Broadband services use special modems to transmit data over the cable television or telephone networks, without affecting your ability to watch TV or make voice calls. Most services are at least ten times as fast as regular dial-up connections.

You are charged a flat monthly rate, so broadband services are good value if you use the Internet for several hours each day. If you're a light to moderate user, a dial-up connection will be cheaper.

For cable-based services, contact the cable television company that serves your area. Broadband services that operate over regular telephone lines are available through Internet service providers.

Internet service providers

An Internet service provider (ISP) enables you to connect to the Internet via a modem and telephone line. Most ISPs also provide basic software and have technical-support people who can help with any problems.

Free services

ISPs such as Freeserve and Virgin Net offer 'free' services – it costs nothing to open an account and there is no monthly fee. However, that doesn't mean you get free access to the Internet. Each time you connect, you're making a telephone call, so you'll notice an increase in your phone bill.

These ISPs fund their services in two ways. First, they get a percentage of your call charges. You don't pay any extra for your calls, but your phone company makes a bit less, because it passes on some of the money to the service provider. Second, if you have problems and need to call the technical-support line, you are charged a premium rate – typically 50p or £1 per minute.

Free services offer a good deal for people who are reasonably comfortable with computers. If you think you'll need help installing and running your Internet software, you might be better off with a subscription-based service.

Subscription-based services

Some services offer one-month free trials for new users. They're a good way to find out what you'll get for your money. If you decide not to continue, ring up and close your account before the trial ends. If you don't, you'll be liable for the monthly fees.

'Regular' ISPs such as Demon Internet and PIPEX charge a monthly fee for their services. This arrangement used to be the norm and still has some advantages. First, subscription-based ISPs offer technical support on local-rate numbers, so you can sort out problems without running up an enormous phone bill. Second, they have more money to invest in infrastructure, so you get a more reliable service. With free services, you may have problems during peak hours. You might have difficulty connecting because all the lines are engaged, or find that everything gets very slow.

Some ISPs offer additional services such as e-mail addresses for all the family, access to a games server, global roaming so you can access the Net while you're overseas, and reception or forwarding of faxes. They may also offer broadband services (see previous page), enabling you to upgrade to a faster connection if your Internet use increases.

On-line services

The third option is to join an on-line service such as AOL or CompuServe. On-line services are similar to regular ISPs, but also have subscriber-only content and private discussion forums. This was a big plus in the days when there weren't many reliable news services on the Web, and business users may still find they offer information that isn't available elsewhere. They also enable parents to provide restricted Internet access for their children.

The other difference is that each on-line service has its own software. They all give you a customised version of Internet Explorer for browsing the Web, but may have special software for connecting to the Internet and sending e-mail. With a free or subscription-based ISP, you can choose your own software.

Choosing an ISP

Once you've decided what type of service provider you require, you need to settle on a particular service. Most Internet magazines publish lists you can refer to. Things to consider include:

1   Level of service. Make sure you'll be getting full Internet access, including e-mail, newsgroups and the Web. Find out what software is supplied, especially if you're considering an on-line service, and whether you can use something else if you don't like it. If you want to create your own Web pages, ask about free Web space.

2   Access numbers. Most service providers use special phone numbers that are charged at the same rate as a local call, no matter where you call from. Some offer special deals that reduce the cost of your calls (see overleaf).

3   Modem speed. Make sure your service provider supports the fastest speed your modem can manage.

4   Subscriber-to-modem ratio. If you choose a service provider that has a lot more subscribers than modems, you'll find it hard to get through. Around 15 subscribers per modem (a ratio of 15:1) is considered adequate.

5   Broadband services. You may only want a regular connection at the moment, but you might need something faster in the

future. Find out whether you'll be able to upgrade to a high-speed cable or ADSL service.

6   Technical support. Find out how much you'll be charged for calls to the helpline, and check the opening hours. A helpline that is only available during the day won't be much good if you're expecting to use the Internet after work or at the weekend. If you don't have much experience with computers, call up and ask a few questions. If the person on the other end can't answer them clearly, try another ISP.

Call charges

Whichever type of service provider you choose, you can run up significant telephone bills, especially if you use the Internet during the day. Over the last few years phone companies and service providers have introduced all sorts of schemes that aim to reduce the overall cost. Some offer lower rates, some give you free calls in the evenings and at weekends, and others let you use the Internet as much as you want for a fixed monthly charge.

Schemes come and go so quickly that it's impossible to make any recommendations. If a deal sounds too good to be true, it probably is – even if it is being trumpeted in the national press. Read all the small print very carefully before you commit yourself. If you have to change phone companies, check the cost of ordinary (voice) calls, make sure you'll get all the services you need, and find out whether you're locked in for a minimum period of time.

Most of the schemes are aimed at people who use the Internet for many hours each week. If you are a light user and can confine your sessions to off-peak periods (evenings and weekends), you won't need to remortgage your house to pay your phone bill. Work out how much you're actually spending on phone calls before you sign up for any of these deals – they won't necessarily save you money.

Getting connected

Make sure your service provider's CD is designed to work with Windows XP.

Setting up your computer to connect to the Internet is usually straightforward. In most cases you get a CD from your Internet service provider, insert it into your PC and follow the on-screen instructions. The software on the disc configures your computer, telling it the phone number to dial and any special settings to use.

You'll probably be asked to choose a user name and password. The user name forms the first part of your e-mail address (see page 136), so choose it carefully. A user name that has your friends in stitches may not seem as amusing when you're applying for a job. Your password should be easy to remember, but difficult for other people to guess (see page 129). Some service providers assign passwords automatically to prevent people from choosing very obvious ones, such as names or birthdates.

The New Connection Wizard

In some cases you'll need to configure your computer by hand. Your service provider may not give you a CD, or you may want more control over the setup process. If you need to reinstall Windows, writing down and re-entering your details is quicker than hunting out a CD you haven't used for months.

Windows XP has a New Connection Wizard that helps you sort out your connection. You'll need the following information:

1   Your service provider's phone number (the modem number, not the number you call to speak to someone)

2   Your user name and password

Later on, you'll also need:

Turn to page 137 to find out how to set up Outlook Express so you can send and receive e-mail. Page 166 explains how to access the news server.

3   Your e-mail address

4   The addresses of your service provider's mail servers (normally there are two)

5   The address of your service provider's news server

It's a good idea to record this information and keep it somewhere safe. If there's anything you don't know, call your service provider.

1. To start the New Connection Wizard, click the Start button and select All Programs>Accessories>Communications>New Connection Wizard

2. Click Next to continue (and again at the end of each step)

If you're setting up an office computer and will be dialling out through a switchboard, fill in the 'If you dial a number to access an outside line...' section of the Location dialogue box.

3. You may be asked for your current location. Select United Kingdom and fill in your area code. Click OK to continue

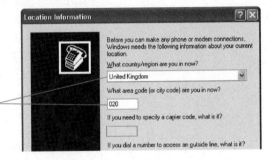

4. When you get back to the New Connection Wizard, select 'Connect to the Internet'

5. Select 'Set up my connection manually'

6. Select 'Connect using a dial-up modem'

7. Fill in the name of your service provider

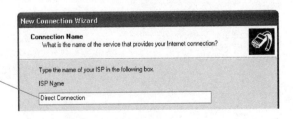

8 Enter your service provider's phone number. Don't forget to include the dialling code

9 Enter your user name and password. The password characters are hidden, so you have to enter it twice to make sure you've got it right

10 Click Finish to create the connection and close the wizard

You can use the Connect To menu option to connect to the Internet – just select your service provider and click the Dial button. However, you don't normally need to do this. Windows will prompt you to connect when you run an Internet program – see overleaf.

11 Click the Start button. You should now have a Connect To option on the right-hand side of the Start menu

Running Internet programs

When you run an Internet program, Windows checks whether you are connected to the Internet. If you aren't, it prompts you to dial your service provider.

1 To run Internet Explorer, click the Start button and select it from the list on the left-hand side of the Start menu

2 The Dial-up Connection dialogue box appears. Your user name and password should be filled in – if not, you'll need to enter them

3 Click the Connect button. You should hear your modem dial and make a connection. Status messages appear at the bottom of the dialogue box

Opening a connection to the Internet is often referred to as 'logging on'. When you're connected, you're said to be 'on-line'. Likewise, 'logging off' means closing the connection. Once that's done, you're 'off-line'.

4 A yellow speech bubble lets you know that the connection has been established

> (i) **Direct Connection is now connected** [X]
> Speed: 31.2 Kbps

5 Internet Explorer displays a Web page like this, or possibly a page from your service provider's Web site

...cont'd

6 You're ready to learn how to browse the Web (see Chapter 2)

You may need to click the arrow button at the left-hand end of the notification area to see the icon. The computers have blue screens when data is flowing up or down your phone line and black screens when the line is idle.

7 When you have finished using the Internet, you need to disconnect. To do this, go to the notification area at the right-hand end of the Windows taskbar. Look for an icon that shows two computers connected together

Don't get the Disconnect and Close buttons confused. When you click the Disconnect button, you end your Internet session. When you click Close, you simply close the dialogue box, without disconnecting your computer from the Internet. To check that you've disconnected correctly, pick up your telephone receiver. You should hear a normal dial tone. If you hear a roaring, hissing noise, you're still connected.

8 Double-click the icon to bring up the Status dialogue box. Click the Disconnect button to close the connection

Direct Connection Status

General | Details

Connection
Status: Connected
Duration: 00:02:46
Speed: 31.2 Kbps

Activity
                   Sent ———   ——— Received
Bytes: 4,484   2,920
Compression: 0 %   0 %
Errors: 0   0

Properties | Disconnect

Close

Fine-tuning your connection

Your connection settings determine how and when Internet Explorer connects to the Internet. You can alter them to make sure it only connects when you want it to, and disconnects automatically when the connection is idle. Some, but not all, of the settings are also applied to other Internet programs.

You can change your settings from Control Panel, too. Select Network and Internet Connections, then Internet Options.

1 Go to Internet Explorer's Tools menu and select Internet Options. Click the Connections tab

2 If you have accounts with several service providers, all the possible connections are listed. Tell Internet Explorer which one to use by selecting it and clicking Set Default

3 Select 'Never dial...' to make connections manually using the Connect To section of the Start menu (see the HOT TIP on page 17). The 'Always dial...' option enables Internet Explorer to make connections as required and is the best choice

4 To fine-tune a connection, select it and click Settings. This opens the dialogue box shown opposite

...cont'd

A proxy server stores copies of all the Web pages that have been viewed by people who use your service provider. If there's a copy of the page you want to see, Internet Explorer can download it from the proxy server more quickly than it could fetch it from the original Web site.

6 If your service provider has a proxy server, select this checkbox and enter the address

7 If your user name or password changes, update your details here

8 If your service provider's phone number changes, click Properties and enter the new one

9 Click Advanced for further options

10 If all your service provider's modems are busy, Internet Explorer tries again. Tell it how many times to redial and how long to wait between attempts

If you enable both the 'Disconnect' options, you won't run up a big phone bill if you forget to log off. Internet Explorer will automatically terminate the connection.

11 Select 'Disconnect if idle' to close the connection if you don't seem to be doing anything. You may want to reduce the idle time

12 Select 'Disconnect when connection may no longer be needed' to end your session if you've closed all your Internet programs

MSN Explorer

This book covers the three principal Internet programs supplied with Windows XP: Internet Explorer, Outlook Express and Windows Messenger. There's also a fourth program, MSN Explorer, which is not covered.

MSN Explorer is an all-in-one Internet program that integrates Web browsing, e-mail and instant messaging. It combines tools from the other three programs with access to Web-based services such as Hotmail (see page 160). It also has a simplified, task-oriented interface.

MSN Explorer is not covered because most people use the other programs. They are very popular and you'll find them installed on most computers. Once you've mastered the version of Internet Explorer supplied with Windows XP, you'll also be able to use the versions on older Windows computers and Apple Macintoshes. Computer magazines, on-line banks and shopping services aim their instructions at people using the standard applications, rather than MSN Explorer.

MSN Explorer is also less powerful and less flexible than the individual applications.

Basic Web browsing

This chapter introduces Internet Explorer and shows you how to customise the interface. It also explains how to enter Web addresses and jump from page to page.

Covers

Chapter Two

Introducing Internet Explorer

To run Internet Explorer, click the Start button and select it from the left-hand side of the Start menu.

Like most Windows programs, it has a title bar, menu bar and toolbars across the top of the window, and a status bar at the bottom. The most important areas of the screen are:

Title bar – shows the name of the page

Menu bar

Standard buttons

Address bar – displays the address, or URL, of the Web page

Links bar – buttons for popular Web sites

If you use a CD from your service provider to configure your Internet connection (see page 15), it may customise Internet Explorer. Don't be alarmed if your version looks slightly different.

Explorer bar – displays extra controls or information

Status bar

Main window, where Web pages are displayed

Customising the toolbars

You can rearrange the Menu bar, Standard buttons, Address bar and Links bar, or turn off some of the bars to increase the size of the main window.

You can also turn toolbars on or off from View>Toolbars.

| To turn off a toolbar, right-click on an empty section of the Standard buttons. A pop-up menu appears. Deselect the toolbar you no longer want to display

2 If there is a checkmark beside Lock the Toolbars, the toolbars are locked. Deselect this option to unlock them

The toolbars have to be at the top of the window. You can't move them to the side or the bottom, or turn them into floating tool palettes.

3 To move a toolbar, use your mouse to grab the grey handle at the left-hand end. Drag it up, down or across

4 You can have several toolbars on the same line

Another way to increase the screen area is by selecting View>Full Screen. If this mode is too minimalist for you, right-click on the Standard buttons to add some of the other toolbars.

5 To expand a toolbar, double-click on its handle. Double-click again to expand it further, and a third time to put it away

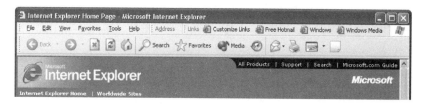

6 If you find you're moving the toolbars by accident, right-click on an empty section and reselect Lock the Toolbars

Customising the Standard buttons

As you become more experienced, you may want to change the Standard buttons. You can add buttons for more advanced features or remove the buttons for tools you don't use. You can also turn off the text labels and reduce the size of the buttons to create a more compact toolbar.

1 To customise the Standard buttons, right-click on an empty section of the toolbar. Select Customize

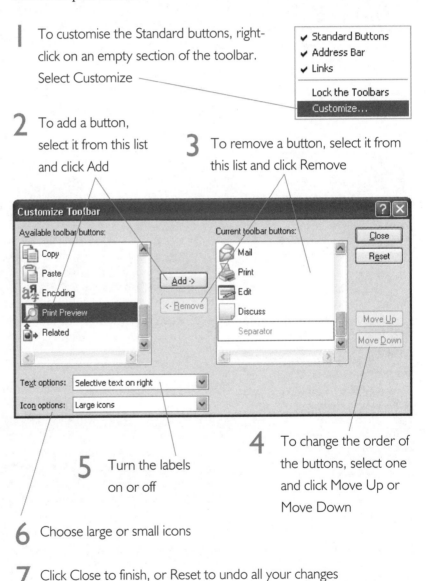

✔ Standard Buttons
✔ Address Bar
✔ Links

Lock the Toolbars
Customize...

Separators are grey lines that can be used to divide the toolbar into sections. Add as many as you need to keep your toolbar tidy.

2 To add a button, select it from this list and click Add

3 To remove a button, select it from this list and click Remove

4 To change the order of the buttons, select one and click Move Up or Move Down

5 Turn the labels on or off

6 Choose large or small icons

7 Click Close to finish, or Reset to undo all your changes

Understanding addresses

 Chapter 5 contains lots of addresses for you to try.

Once you're comfortable with Internet Explorer's interface, you're ready to go somewhere. Every page on the Web has a unique address, otherwise known as a Uniform Resource Locator (URL). You've probably seen some Web addresses in newspapers and magazines and on television.

The URL for Microsoft's Internet Explorer Web page is:

 A page is a single Web document. Some are quite long – use the scroll bar to move down them. A site is a collection of related pages, and the server is the computer on which all the documents are stored.

The 'http:' indicates that this is a Web page

This section tells your browser which folder the page is stored in

This is the name of the server where the page is stored

This is the name of the document that describes the page

 Web addresses never contain spaces, but they can include hyphens and some other punctuation. Sometimes they are case-sensitive, so if you see a capital 'T' in an address, don't type a lower-case 't'.

Internet Explorer assumes you are looking for a Web page, so you don't have to type the `http://` at the beginning. If you're looking for the main page of a company's site, you can also leave out everything after the first single slash. To find the main page of Microsoft's Web site, you would enter: `www.microsoft.com`

Interpreting Web addresses

Most server names have three or four sections:

`www.microsoft.com`
`www.bbc.co.uk`

 You don't have to know how to decode Web addresses – you just have to type them correctly. However, if you know how the names are constructed, you can spot mistakes and work out how to fix them.

The last section (`.com`) or last two sections (`.co.uk`) tell you about the owner of the address. The middle section (`microsoft` or `bbc`) is usually the owner's name. Collectively, the last two or three sections are known as a 'domain name'. The first section (www) is used to distinguish between different servers belonging to the same organisation. It's known as a 'host name'.

The rules for the last section (or sections) are confusing. They reflect the haphazard evolution of the Internet, so don't bother trying to work out the logic. The most common single-section endings are:

There are three 'global' top-level domains that are reserved for US organisations. They are `.edu` *(education),* `.gov` *(government) and* `.mil` *(military).*

`.com`	*com*mercial entity (but also used by individuals)
`.org`	*org*anisation (usually non-profit)
`.net`	Inter*net*-related business (such as an ISP)
`.int`	*int*ernational body (such as the United Nations)

These endings are known as 'global top-level domains', because the owner can be based anywhere in the world. Seven new ones are currently being added: `.aero` (air transport), `.biz` (businesses), `.coop` (co-operatives), `.info` (information), `.museum` (museums), `.name` (individuals) and `.pro` (professionals).

For a complete list of country codes, visit the Web site of the Internet Assigned Numbers Authority (IANA), at: `http://www.iana.org/cctld/cctld.htm`

Two-section endings consist of an organisation code and a country code: `.uk` (United Kingdom), `.fr` (France), `.de` (Germany), `.au` (Australia), `.za` (South Africa) and so on. The organisation codes differ from country to country. In the UK, the most common endings are:

`.co.uk`	equivalent to `.com`
`.org.uk`	equivalent to `.org`
`.net.uk`	equivalent to `.net`
`.ac.uk`	academic institution (but not a school, which would have a `.sch.uk` address)
`.gov.uk`	government

Other addresses

You may also see URLs that don't begin with `http://`. These take you to other types of Internet site:

URL begins	Type of site
`https://`	Secure Web site (see page 127)
`mailto:`	E-mail address (see page 136)
`news:`	Usenet newsgroup (see page 164)

Entering an address

If you know the address of the Web page you wish to visit, enter it into Internet Explorer. There are three ways to do this:

If you type 'ineasysteps' (without the single quotes) and press Ctrl+Enter, 'www.' and '.com' are added for you.

1 Type the address into the Address bar, then click the Go button or press the Enter key. Internet Explorer finds and displays the page

2 Once you've visited a few sites, Internet Explorer tries to anticipate your typing. If you see the right address in the drop-down list, click on it. You don't have to press Enter

You can also click the arrow at the right-hand end of the Address bar for a list of addresses you've entered recently. This list only shows addresses you've typed yourself.

3 If you have turned off the Address bar, select Open from the File menu or press Ctrl+O. Both actions bring up the Open dialogue box. Type an address, or select one from the list. Click OK

If you don't want Internet Explorer to complete your addresses, turn this feature off under Tools>Internet Options> Content>AutoComplete.

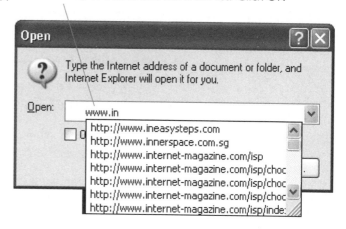

Problems you may have

The Internet is constantly evolving: sites come and go and servers are moved or upgraded. It's also subject to its fair share of bugs and bad connections, so sometimes Internet Explorer gives you an error message instead of displaying the page you want to see:

Don't be surprised if you see something quite different. Some Web sites have their own error messages with more specific information.

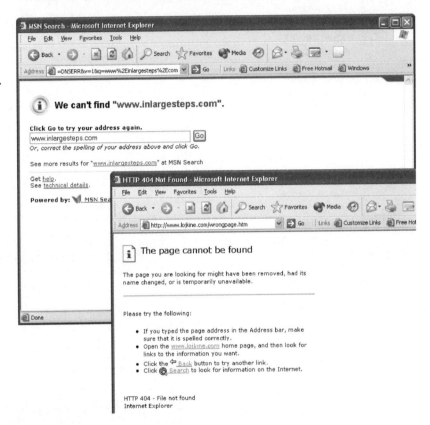

The vast majority of errors arise because:

1   You've typed the address incorrectly. Try again, checking the address carefully before you click Go or press Enter.

2   The computer where the page is stored is temporarily out of action. Try again in a few hours' time.

3   The page you want has moved. If this is the case, Internet Explorer displays the address of the main page of the Web site. Click it and try to find the page from there.

Using links

If you could only get to Web pages by typing in their URLs, browsing the Web would be time-consuming and tedious. Fortunately there's a much easier way to get about: links.

Almost every Web page is linked to anything from one to a hundred or more other pages. Links are usually indicated by coloured, underlined text, and you move to the linked page by clicking this text. For example:

Links can also take you to another section of the same page. For example, many long pages have a list of the major subheadings at the top. Clicking on a heading takes you to the relevant subsection.

1 Here's a page from the Yahoo! Web directory (see page 78). If you click the blue, underlined text that says 'Arts & Humanities'…

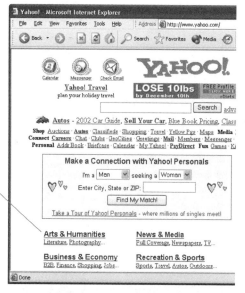

2 …you are taken to this page, which lists the Arts & Humanities subcategories. Choose a topic and click again to go to another page

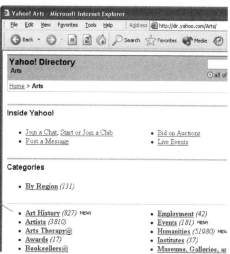

You can tell when the mouse pointer is over a link, because it changes into a pointing hand ✋. While you're pointing, check the Status bar. You should see the name of the file or site at the other end of the link. The linked text usually changes colour after you've clicked it, so you can see where you've been.

Images can also be used as links – see page 41.

New windows

When you click on a link, the new page normally replaces the original one. If you want to display both pages at once, you can load the second one into a new window. This trick is useful when you want to compare two pages, take a detour or keep material on the screen for reference.

Sometimes clicking on a link opens a new window automatically. This isn't a mistake – the designer of the original site is hoping you'll explore the linked page, then close the new window and go back to where you were.

1 Suppose you've found an interesting Web site in Yahoo!'s listings. You want to explore it, but you also want to keep the directory on your screen. Hold down Shift when you click the link, or right-click the link and select Open in New Window from the pop-up menu

2 The linked site opens in its own window

Retracing your steps

Although people talk about the 'information superhighway', browsing the Web is more like exploring the back streets of a market town: there are lots of directions to head in and it's easy to get lost. However, it's also easy to retrace your steps.

| To return to the page you just left, click the Back button or press Alt+Left Arrow

You can use the History bar to return to any page you've visited in the last two or three weeks – see page 73.

2 To go back several pages, click the arrow to the right of the Back button. Select the page you want to revisit from the pop-up list

3 Once you've gone back a few pages, you may want to go forward again. Click the Forward button or press Alt+Right Arrow. If you want to go forward several pages, click the arrow to the right of the Forward button

4 If you get lost, you can start again by clicking the Home button or pressing Alt+Home. This takes you to your Home Page – the page Internet Explorer looks for each time you run it. It's usually a page from your service provider's Web site, or a Microsoft page, but you can change it to anything you like – see page 67

Stop and Refresh

If the Internet is busy, Web pages can take a long time to arrive, so Internet Explorer lets you end tedious downloads. You can then go somewhere else, or hope for a better connection and try again.

The logo in the top right corner is animated when a page is downloading and becomes static when the transfer is complete. You can click on links as soon as you see the text – you don't have to wait for the rest of the page to arrive.

1   To abort a download, click the Stop button, select View>Stop or press Esc. Internet Explorer gives up fetching the page

2   If you change your mind and want to see the rest of a half-downloaded page, click the Refresh button, select View>Refresh or press F5 to reload the page. You should also click Refresh if you think Internet Explorer isn't displaying a page correctly

3   You can use Refresh to make sure you're seeing the very latest version of a page. For example, pages showing sports results may be updated every few minutes, but the new data won't necessarily be sent to your computer. Sites that work this way usually tell you to 'reload often'

Getting help

Internet Explorer has a Web-style Help file that's handy if you need to check something while you're on-line.

The Contents section only lists some of the topics. If you're looking for information about a specific feature, it's best to go straight to the Index. Only use the Search section (covered overleaf) if the Index has failed you. It finds more topics, but many of them only mention your keyword in passing.

1 To open the Help file, go to Help>Contents and Index

2 Click a chapter title, then select a topic. The text is displayed on the right

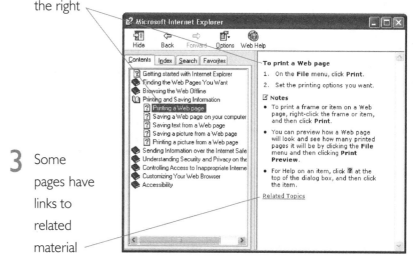

3 Some pages have links to related material

4 If you can't find the information you want, click the Index tab

5 Type in a keyword

6 Select a topic and click Display

...cont'd

You can access the Support section of Microsoft's Web site by selecting Help>Online Support. However, most of the information you'll find there is aimed at experts.

7 Still need more information? Click the Search tab

8 Enter your keyword again

9 Click the List Topics button

10 This time you see all the topics that mention your keyword. Select a topic and click Display to read about it in the right-hand pane

Adding a topic to the Favorites list is like creating a Favorite for a Web site – see Chapter 4.

11 To record the location of this topic, click the Favorites tab

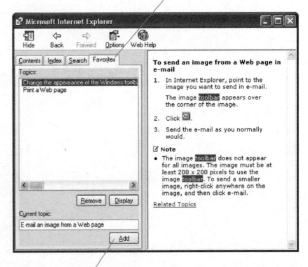

12 Click the Add button to add the topic to the Favorites list. Over time it'll evolve into a list of shortcuts for all your favourite topics

Working with Web pages

This chapter explains what to do when you come across images, sounds, video clips, program files and interactive Web pages. It also shows you how to save and/or print Web pages so you can refer to them off-line.

Covers

Chapter Three

Understanding Web pages

Web pages start out as unformatted text files – the type of file your word processor produces when you save a document as 'text' or 'plain text'. The designer then specifies how the page should look by inserting pairs of 'tags'. To emphasise a phrase by displaying it in bold type, for example, they insert a 'bold on' tag at the beginning and a 'bold off' tag at the end. When you download the file, Internet Explorer reads the tags and adds the formatting.

To see what an HTML file really looks like, open a Web page and select View>Source. Internet Explorer transfers the file to Notepad, which displays the tags (look for things in angle <> brackets) as well as the text.

This system is known as HyperText Mark-up Language (HTML). As well as enabling Web designers to format their pages, it makes it possible to include references to other files. For example, links are created using a pair of tags that say, 'If someone clicks anywhere between here (link on) and here (link off), load file xyz.' It might not sound very exciting, but without the ability to include these instructions in the pages, the whole thing would fall apart. You'd have to know the location of every single page instead of jumping from one to the next.

Additional uses for tags

Tags can also be used to tell the browser to download additional files and insert them into the text. This is how the images arrive: Internet Explorer reads the HTML file, finds an instruction that tells it to 'insert image abc', fetches the image file, works out how everything should look and displays the page. This is why the text often appears first: until you download the HTML file, Internet Explorer doesn't even know there should be pictures.

Unless you want to create your own Web pages, you don't need to worry about the ins and outs of HTML. However, it's worth remembering that the pictures are stored separately from the text, as are sounds, animations and video clips.

Images

Before the Web was invented, the Internet was a text-based medium. You could access useful information from around the globe and many interesting discussions were held, but it all looked about as exciting as pages from the phone book, so no-one wanted to put the Internet on television. It was clever, but it wasn't pretty.

If you see an icon with a red cross ☒ where an image should be, Internet Explorer either can't find or can't display the image file.

The addition of images changed all that. They make the Web colourful and interesting, add personality and give it a friendly face. They're used to illustrate news stories and travel guides, to liven up personal Web pages, to show you products in on-line shops, and to create fancy buttons and headings. The Web wouldn't be the same without them.

Images can be displayed as part of a Web page, or on their own. In the first case, Internet Explorer slots the picture(s) into the text, according to the Web designer's instructions. In the second, it simply displays the picture in the main window. To find out whether you're looking at a whole page or just a single image, look at the Address bar. If the address ends in .gif, .jpg, .jpeg or .png, you're viewing an image.

To turn an image into Windows wallpaper, right-click on it, then select Set as Background from the pop-up menu.

Entire
Web page

An image
on its own

...cont'd

Holding the mouse pointer over something, without clicking, is know as 'hovering' or 'pointing'.

The Image toolbar doesn't appear when you hover the mouse pointer over very small images.

If you don't find the Image toolbar useful, you can turn it off. Next time it appears, right-click on it and select Disable Image Toolbar. To turn it on again, go to Tools>Internet Options. Click the Advanced tab and scroll down to the Multimedia section. Select the 'Enable Image Toolbar' checkbox.

Image toolbar

If you hold the mouse pointer over an image, without clicking, a small toolbar may appear. It has four buttons that enable you to do things with the image.

1 Save the image

2 Print the image

3 Attach the image to an e-mail message so you can send it to a friend (see Chapter 8)

4 Open the My Pictures folder. You can copy the image into this folder by dragging it across with the mouse

When you view an image on its own, rather than as part of a Web page, a second control may appear in the bottom right corner. This means Internet Explorer has resized the image to make it fit into the main window.

1 Click to expand the image to its normal size. Use the scroll bars to move around

2 Click again to make the image fit in the window

Images as links

Images aren't just used to make the pages pretty; they can also help you get from one to the next. The four most common types of image link are:

You can find out whether an image is a link by moving the mouse pointer over it. If it changes to a pointing hand, just as it does over a text link (see page 32), clicking will take you to another page.

1   *Buttons* – many Web sites use icons and toolbars to help you navigate. For example, the Yahoo! Web directory (see page 78) has buttons that take you to special sections of the site.

2   *Text* – when Web designers want to use a special font, create fancy text effects or combine text with graphics, they have to save the text in an image file. The result doesn't look like regular linked text, but it may function the same way.

3   *Image maps* – some images contain more than one link. For example, the BBC Web site (see page 87) included this map in its coverage of Wimbledon. When you clicked on one of the black areas, you got more information about the selected court or building.

4   *Thumbnails* – because large images take a long time to download, Web designers often show you small preview versions first. If you visit the Internet Movie Database (see page 86) and look at a photo gallery, you'll get a page like this. Click the thumbnail images to see larger versions of the photographs.

Photo gallery for Monsters, Inc.

Studio Stills

Click on a below to see it in a larger size.

Still photographs of "Monsters, Inc.

Sounds and videos

Some Web sites have background music that plays automatically when you download a page. If a tune is getting on your nerves, click Stop to halt the playback.

It's more common for audio and video files to be linked to the page, so you can decide whether you want to play them.

To save a sound or video clip onto your hard disk, right-click the link that leads to it and select Save Target As. This doesn't always work – some files can't be saved.

1 To play a sound or video clip, such as these videos from NASA's Web site (see page 100), click the link that leads to the file. You may need to select your connection speed

April 19, 2001 --- This is a vid Endeavour for STS-100, a mi This video tracks the orbiter first three minutes of flight. V the Canadian-built Space St: (SSRMS). In addition, Endea Purpose Logistics Module, w equipment and supplies for t

Media Player Format - 28K / 56K

Real Video Format - 28K / 56K

2 If Internet Explorer can play the clip, it offers to do so. Click Yes to proceed

Playback begins quickly because this video clip is stored in a streaming format – see page 44.

3 Internet Explorer displays the Media bar to the left of the main window and downloads the clip. It starts playing automatically

4 Use the Play/Pause and Stop buttons to control the playback

5 Use the slider to adjust the volume

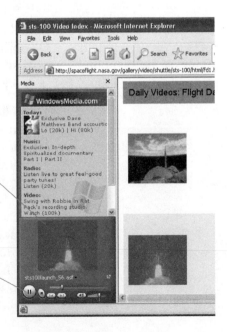

6 If you'd rather play the clip in a separate window, click the Undock Player button

7 Playback continues in the new window. To transfer the video clip back to the Media bar, click the Redock Player button

If Internet Explorer can play a sound or video file, it does. If it can't, it may automatically transfer the file to another program – see Chapter 6. Sometimes it can't do that either, usually because you haven't got the required software. If you're having problems playing sounds or videos from a particular Web site, see if there's an information page that tells you what software you need and where to get it from.

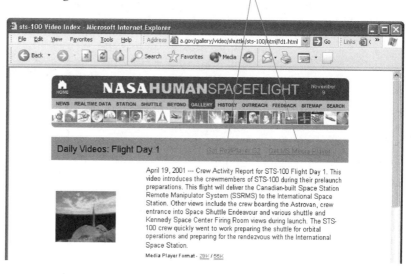

Streaming sound and video

Some sound and video files have to be downloaded before you can play them back. This can take a long time. For example, a four-minute song saved in the MP3 format might take 16 minutes to download. If it were saved in the Windows Audio (.wav) format, you'd have to wait even longer.

Some Web sites provide several versions of each sound file or video, optimised for streaming at different speeds. Pick the one that matches the speed of your connection.

Streaming sound and video formats were invented to speed things up. They are compressed so each minute of sound or video takes a minute to download. This means you can play the 'stream' as it downloads, rather than afterwards.

Streaming formats can't compete with traditional sound and video files for audio and picture quality, because a lot of data has to be stripped out to keep downloading and playback in sync. However, you get to see or hear something seconds after you click on a link.

Streaming is used to transmit radio and television shows over the Internet, and for live 'Webcasts' of special events. It can also be used for prerecorded material. For example, CD merchants such as CD Universe (see page 93) often let you listen to sample tracks so you can make sure you're buying the right disc.

You need the latest version of Windows Media Player to get the best out of Windows Media files. Get it from: `http://www.microsoft.com/windows/windowsmedia/en/default.asp`

Common streaming formats include RealAudio, RealVideo, QuickTime, Windows Media Audio and Windows Media Video. Internet Explorer can play Windows Media files, but you need extra software for the others – see Chapter 6.

Downloading program files

You can download lots of software from the Internet, including public domain and shareware programs, demo versions of commercial software and add-ons for many programs. Internet Explorer enables you to fetch and run these files in a single operation, but you'll almost always want to save them onto your hard disk instead. You can experiment with your new software once you've disconnected from the Internet.

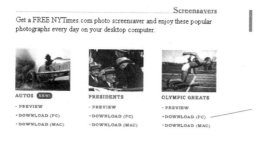

1 To download a program file, such as this screensaver from *The New York Times* (see page 82), click the relevant link

There's always a chance that a downloaded program might contain a virus. See page 121 for advice.

2 Internet Explorer asks whether you want to open (run) the file or save it onto your hard disk. Click the Save button

3 The standard Save As dialogue box appears. Select a folder and click the Save button

4 The file is downloaded onto your hard disk – this often takes several minutes. You can continue browsing or switch to another program and carry on working

5 Once the download is complete, you have three options. Click Open to run the program straightaway

6 Click Open Folder to find the file on your hard disk

7 Or, click Close to close the dialogue box and go on with something else. Don't forget to go back and deal with your new program later on!

Compressed files

Web designers often use compression programs to 'archive' the program files linked to their pages. Creating an archive packs everything – setup utility, documentation, help files and the program itself – into a single, neat package. The archive is substantially smaller than the original group of files, so it downloads more quickly.

A file extension consists of a dot (.) and three extra characters at the end of the filename. The extension tells you what kind of file you're dealing with. For example, a file called readme.txt is a text file. Windows normally hides file extensions, but it's often useful to display them. To do this, open Control Panel. Go to the Tools menu and select Folder Options, then click the View tab. Under Advanced Settings, deselect the 'Hide extensions for known file types' option.

The most popular compression programs produce archives with a .zip extension. Follow the instructions on the previous two pages to save them on to your hard disk.

Once you have downloaded a .zip file, you'll need to decompress or 'unzip' it.

1 Open the folder containing the .zip file. Double-click it

2 Windows displays the contents of the file. To unzip it, click 'Extract all files'

3 The Extraction wizard helps you unpack the files into a new folder

You'll also come across other types of archive. Self-extracting archives have an .exe extension and unzip themselves automatically when you double-click the original file. Archives with names ending in .hqx, .sit, .sea, .gz, .Z, .tar or .gtar contain Apple Macintosh or Unix files. It's unlikely you'll be able to use the contents of these archives, so it's best to avoid them.

Interactive Web pages

So far this chapter has dealt with material that can be attached to Web pages: images, sounds, videos and program files. However, interactive elements such as buttons to click and text boxes to fill in are usually created by adding instructions to the HTML document that describes the Web page.

Scripts

It's possible for a malicious programmer to use scripts to access private information or cause problems on your computer – see page 125 for more on this and similar hazards.

A script is a set of instructions that is included in a Web page. You don't see the script on the screen, but it tells Internet Explorer what to do when you click a button or enter some text. Scripts are used to display dialogue boxes, carry out simple calculations and add special effects such as scrolling messages. They can also change the formatting of a Web page at a specified time, or in response to your mouse movements, mouse clicks and keystrokes. Items can appear or disappear, move around, change colour and so on. It's even possible to produce simple games and utilities.

You're most likely to notice scripts when something goes wrong. If Internet Explorer encounters an instruction it doesn't understand, it displays an error message. Sometimes you can ignore the error – you may be able to get all the information you need, even though the page isn't being displayed properly. If you can't, all you can do is e-mail the site's designer with details of the problem.

Forms

Forms enable you to enter keywords into search engines, fill out questionnaires and register for Web sites. However, they aren't all dry and serious. They are also used for interactive gadgets such as automatic letter writers.

Forms are just like dialogue boxes, except the text boxes, drop-down lists, radio buttons and checkboxes are part of the Web page. Once you have filled in the blanks, you click a button to send the data back to the Web server. You'll get a response – another Web page – a few seconds later.

Here's a form from Railtrack's Web site (see page 96):

Text boxes

Radio buttons

Drop-down list

When you fill in your requirements and click the Submit button, you're given a list of suitable trains.

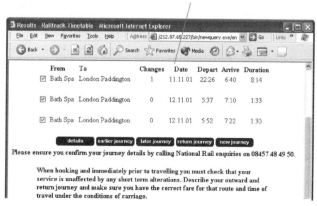

AutoComplete

Internet Explorer can remember all the things you've typed into forms and anticipate your typing.

AutoComplete only works when Internet Explorer knows what type of information a box should contain. It won't try to enter your name into an address box.

The first time you fill in a form, you're asked if you want to activate this feature. Click Yes if you do

2 Internet Explorer starts remembering your entries. When you type a 'B' into Railtrack's Destination box, Internet Explorer lists the 'B' place names you've entered previously. Click the correct one to fill in the box

You can turn off AutoComplete if you don't find it helpful. You can also clear the list of words and start again.

Select Tools > Internet Options and click the Content tab. Click the AutoComplete button

2 Deselect any or all of the AutoComplete options

To delete an individual entry from the list associated with a particular text box, wait for the drop-down list to appear, then highlight the entry and press Delete.

3 Click Clear Forms to make Internet Explorer forget all the words you've typed into forms

Site registration

Some of the large commercial sites require you to register for access. Usually the company wants to find out what kind of people visit the site so it can sell advertising. Knowing who you are also enables the Web site to personalise its service. For example, it may display a list of pages that have been added since the last time you logged on.

On-line shops such as Amazon.co.uk (see page 93) may ask you to register when you make your first purchase. They keep your details on file so you can check out more quickly on subsequent visits. Instead of re-entering your address each time you buy something, you just confirm that the shop has the correct details.

amazon.co.uk
HELP DESK

Registration

New to Amazon? Register Below

My name is: Mary Lojkine

My e-mail address: mary@lojkine.com

Protect your information with a password
This will be your only Amazon.co.uk password.

Enter a new password: ●●●●●●●●

Type it again: ●●●●●●●●

Continue ▶

Don't use the user name and password supplied by your service provider. Anyone who knows these details can use your Internet account, so keep them secret.

Registration involves filling in a form and selecting a user name and password. It's a good idea to write down your passwords and keep them somewhere safe, because you'll end up with more than you can possibly remember.

Internet Explorer may ask if it should remember the password for you. Whether this is a good idea depends on the nature of the Web site and the number of people who use your computer. See Chapter 7 for more on passwords and Internet security.

Frames

Frames divide the main window into two or more 'panes' that can be scrolled or updated separately. They enable Web designers to display several pages at once. Frames are often used to keep menus within easy reach.

Most pages that use frames have grey dividing bars between the sections, but it's possible for the designer to make the divisions invisible.

Clicking a link in one of the frames can change its contents, or change the contents of the other frames, or take you to a another Web page. For example, About.com (see page 78) recommends sites on a wide range of subjects. When you click one of the links, Internet Explorer's main window is split into two frames. The bottom one displays the recommended Web site. The top one enables you to return to About.com with a single click.

Top frame: About.com

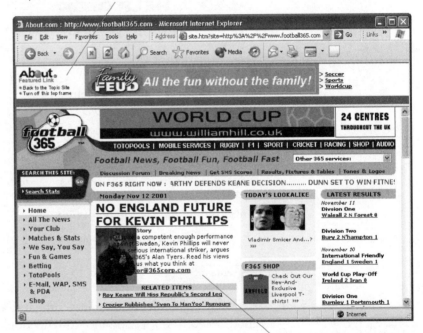

Bottom frame: Football365
(see page 91)

Saving Web pages

Sometimes you'll come across a Web page with information you might want to refer to in the future. Saving it onto your hard disk enables you to reload it whenever you want, without the expense of logging on and downloading it again.

See page 87 for more about the BBC Web site.

1 To save a Web page, select File> Save As. This brings up the Save As dialogue box

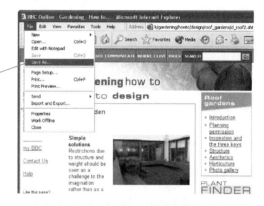

Don't forget that material on the Web is protected by copyright. Keeping copies for personal reference is unlikely to get you into trouble, but you mustn't reuse or redistribute text, images, sounds or videos without permission.

2 Choose a folder and name the file

3 Select 'Web Page, complete' to save the text and the pictures as separate files

4 Or, select 'Web Archive, single file' to store everything in one file

5 Or, select 'Web Page, HTML only' to save the text and the formatting instructions

6 Or, select 'Text File' to just save the text, without the formatting

7 Click Save

8 'Web Page, complete' produces an .htm file for the page and a folder full of picture files

9 'Web Archive, single file' produces a file with an .mht extension

10 Either way, you can load the page back into Internet Explorer by double-clicking on the file. Alternatively, select Open from Internet Explorer's File menu. Click the Browse button to find the file

Printing Web pages

If you're gathering information for a report or project, printing Web pages can be more convenient than saving them. You don't end up with a hard disk full of Web pages and you can scribble notes in the margins or highlight important passages.

You can also click the Print button on the toolbar, but you'll bypass the Print dialogue box

1 To print the current page, pull down the File menu and select Print. Alternatively, press Ctrl+P

If you're only interested in a couple of paragraphs of text, highlight them with the mouse before you go to File>Print. In Step 2, choose 'Selection'.

2 Decide whether to print the whole document or specified pages (see overleaf)

3 If the page has frames (see page 52), click the Options tab

The easiest way to print a single frame is to right-click within it and select Print from the pop-up menu. That way you'll know the correct frame is selected.

4 Decide whether to print all the frames, or just the selected one (the one you clicked in most recently)

5 Click the Print button to print the page

Print Preview

Because Web pages are designed to be viewed on a monitor, they don't always print the way you expect them to. If you use Internet Explorer's Print Preview function, you get more control over the output. Sometimes it's enough to make the difference between wasting paper and producing a useful printout.

1 To preview your printout, select File > Print Preview

To decode the header and footer codes in the Setup box, click the Help button ❓ in the top right corner, then click on the Header or Footer settings.

2 To change the margins, header, footer and/or page orientation, click the Setup button 🖼

3 Use these controls to move from page to page or zoom in or out

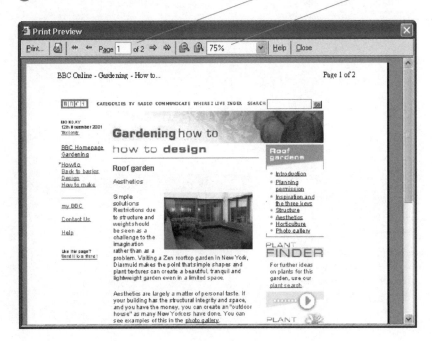

4 Once you're happy, click the Print button.

Print Preview lets you see which pages contain useful information. When you click Print, you can use the 'Print range' options (Step 2, previous page) to omit the others.

Finding your way

There are over a billion Web pages and it's easy to lose your way as you jump from one to the next. This chapter explains how to use Favorites, Shortcuts and the Links bar to keep track of the ones you visit regularly. It also shows you how to find information on the Web.

Covers

Chapter Four

Creating Favorites

As you explore the Web, you'll often come across sites you'll want to visit again in the future. Rather than writing down the address, add the site to Internet Explorer's Favorites menu.

You can also right-click on the page and select Add to Favorites from the pop-up menu. Right-click on a link to create a Favorite for the Web page at the other end.

1 To create a Favorite for the current page, select Add to Favorites from the Favorites menu

The 'Make available offline' option is covered on page 63.

2 Check the name – you may want to change it to something shorter or clearer. Click OK to create the Favorite

See page 86 to find out more about the Internet Movie Database.

3 You can return to this page whenever you want, simply by selecting it from the Favorites menu

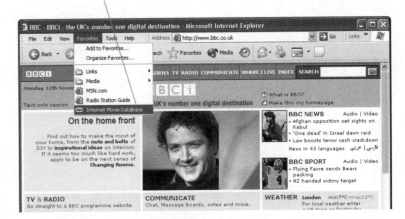

Managing Favorites

Once you have 15–20 Favorites, you'll need to start organising them into folders. This creates submenus and makes it easier to find the one you want.

1 Select Organize Favorites from the Favorites menu

You'll already have a Links folder (see page 66) and a Media folder.

2 Click the Create Folder button

3 Type in a name and press Enter

You can also drag Favorites to the correct folders.

4 Select a Favorite that needs to be relocated into the new folder. Internet Explorer displays its details on the left

5 Click Move to Folder

6 Select the folder and click OK

7 Click Close to finish organising your Favorites

...cont'd

To save a new Favorite straight into a folder, click the Create in>> button (see Step 2 on page 58). Select the folder, then click OK.

8 Your Favorites menu now has submenus. To access them, hold the mouse pointer over the folder's menu entry until the submenu appears

You can also reorganise your Favorites by dragging them around with the mouse. Open the menu, or a submenu, and point to an entry with the mouse. Press and hold the left mouse button, then drag the Favorite or folder to a new location. You can move it to a particular position by looking out for the black divider that appears when the mouse pointer is between two items.

9 To sort your Favorites and folders into alphabetical order, open the Favorites menu and right-click on it. Select Sort by Name from the pop-up menu

10 Repeat for each of your submenus

Favorites bar

The Favorites bar gives you another way to access your Favorites. It's more convenient than the menu, but takes up quite a lot of the main window.

1 Click the Favorites button to open the Favorites bar

2 Click a folder to see a list of Favorites. Click again to close the folder

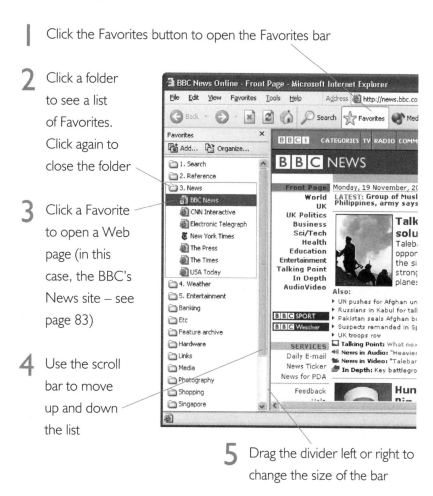

3 Click a Favorite to open a Web page (in this case, the BBC's News site – see page 83)

4 Use the scroll bar to move up and down the list

5 Drag the divider left or right to change the size of the bar

6 Click the Favorites button again to close the Favorites bar. You can also click the cross [x] in the top right corner of the bar

Exporting Favorites

Your Favorites are stored in individual files on your hard disk, in a special section of the Documents and Settings folder. The Import/Export Wizard packs them all into a single file that you can copy on to a back-up disk, transfer to another computer or give to a friend.

1 To export your Favorites, go to File>Import and Export. The Import/Export Wizard appears. Click Next to proceed (and again after each step)

2 Select 'Export Favorites'

Exporting the Favorites from a submenu is useful when you have a collection of Favorites on a particular subject. To share those Favorites with a friend, export the submenu and give them the file.

3 Select the Favorites folder to export all your Favorites, or an individual folder to export the Favorites from a submenu

To move your Favorites to another PC, export them, then copy the file to the new computer. Run Internet Explorer and go to File>Import and Export. Select the 'Import Favorites' option.

4 Select the 'Export to a File or Address' option. The default settings create a file called 'bookmark.htm' in My Documents

5 Click Next, then Finish, to create the file

6 You can open the file in Internet Explorer. Go to File>Open, then click the Browse button to locate it

Browsing pages off-line

If you have a laptop, you may want to download pages from your favourite news site while you eat breakfast, then read them on the train. Internet Explorer can copy material from selected Web pages into a folder on your hard disk, enabling you to access the information without reconnecting to the Internet.

1 To mark the pages that you want to download, go to Favorites> Organize Favorites

2 Select the Web site you're interested in, then select the 'Make available offline' checkbox

3 The front page of a news site often gives you the headlines, then provides links to the stories. To fetch the linked pages, click Properties

4 Click the Download tab

Don't go more than one link deep unless the site has very few links.

5 Set 'Download pages...' to one link deep

6 Decide whether to follow links to other servers

If in doubt, follow external links and don't set a limit for the site. You can come back and change these options later if there's a problem.

7 If you're short of disk space, set a limit for this site

8 Click OK. Repeat steps 2–7 for any other sites you want to download

...cont'd

Selecting the 'Make available offline' checkbox marks a site for download. However, the files aren't fetched until you tell Internet Explorer to synchronise the pages on your hard disk with the ones on the Internet (it does this spontaneously when you first select a site, but you'll need to synchronise manually thereafter).

Synchronising

When you synchronise your computer, Internet Explorer checks whether the pages have been updated and downloads new material.

1 Go to the Tools menu and select Synchronize

2 Click the checkboxes of the sites you want to download

3 Click Synchronize

4 Internet Explorer checks for updates and downloads any pages that have changed

5 When it has finished, log off

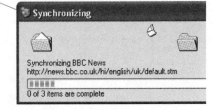

> **HOT TIP**
>
> *The pages you download are stored in the Temporary Internet Files folder, otherwise known as the 'cache'. You may need to allocate extra space to this folder if you want to view a lot of pages off-line.*
>
> *To do this, go to Tools> Internet Options and click the General tab. In the Temporary Internet Files section, click Settings. Move the slider to increase the capacity of this folder.*

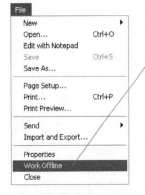

6 Go to the File menu and select Work Offline (this stops Internet Explorer from trying to connect to the Internet)

7 Use the Favorites menu or Favorites bar to call up the pages you've downloaded. They'll have red stars on their icons

Internet Shortcuts

An Internet Shortcut is a Favorite that lives on your Windows desktop, rather than in the Favorites menu. Double-clicking on it runs Internet Explorer, connects you to the Internet and takes you to the specified page.

Internet Shortcuts are useful for sites you visit frequently. For example, you could use a Shortcut to the BBC's News site (see page 83) to start Internet Explorer first thing in the morning. Later in the day you might want to use a search engine or go straight to a sports or entertainment site.

If you can see some of your desktop alongside Internet Explorer's window, you can make Shortcuts using the 'page' icon at the left-hand end of the Address bar. Drag it on to the desktop to make a Shortcut for the page.

1 To create an Internet Shortcut, right-click on the background of the Web page and select Create Shortcut from the pop-up menu. Alternatively, go to File>Send>Shortcut To Desktop

2 A dialogue box appears. Click OK to confirm the creation of the Shortcut

3 The Shortcut is placed on your desktop. To give it a better name, click on it once, wait a couple of seconds and then click again. Type in a short, descriptive name

4 Double-click the Shortcut to start Internet Explorer and load the specified page (if Internet Explorer is already running, double-clicking the Shortcut just takes you to the page)

Links bar

The Links bar provides another way to access your favourite sites. When you install Internet Explorer, it contains buttons for sites selected by Microsoft or your service provider. You can replace these with your own top choices.

1 If you don't find the default links useful, right-click on them and select Delete from the pop-up menu

You can also make a button for the current page by dragging the page icon from the Address bar to the Links bar.

2 There are several ways to create buttons.
To add the page you're currently viewing, select Add to

Favorites from the Favorites menu. Click the Create in<< button and select the Links folder

Why do some sites have fancy icons? This is up to the Web designer – if they create a special icon, Internet Explorer uses it. To change an icon, right-click on it and select Properties. Click the Change Icon button and choose another design.

3 Another option is to open the Favourites bar and drag a Favorite on to the Links bar. Place it between the existing buttons – a black divider appears when the mouse is in the right place

4 If you add more sites than Internet Explorer can display, an arrow button appears at the right-hand end of the bar. Click it to see the rest of the buttons in a list

Home Page

Internet Explorer looks for the Home Page each time you run it. You're also taken to this page when you click the Home button or press Alt+Home.

The default Home Page is usually one of your service provider's Web pages, although you may be taken to one of Microsoft's Web pages instead. You don't have to stick with the default setting, though – you can change the Home Page to any page you visit often or find useful, such as a news site or Web directory.

1 To change your Home Page, browse to the site you'd like to use. Select Tools>Internet Options and click the General tab

2 Click Use Current to change your Home Page

> **Internet Options** [?] [X]
>
> General | Security | Privacy | Content | Connections | Programs | Advanced
>
> ┌─ Home page ─────────────────────────────
> │ You can change which page to use for your home page.
> │ Address: http://www.yahoo.com/
> │ [Use Current] [Use Default] [Use Blank]

3 Or, click Use Default to revert to the Home Page that was specified when you installed Internet Explorer

4 Or, click Use Blank if you often want to run Internet Explorer without connecting to the Internet. It will load a blank page from your hard disk instead of running the connection software

Searching the Internet

Browsing aimlessly around the Internet is easy – you keep clicking links until you come across something interesting. More often than not, though, you'll be looking for specific information. If you were in a library, you'd consult the catalogue; on the Internet, you turn to the organisations who devote their time to indexing the Web.

There are three types of index. Directories list sites by topic and subtopic, enabling you to focus in on the area of interest gradually. If you are looking for an explanation of Albert Einstein's Theory of Relativity, for example, you select Science, and then Physics, Relativity and so on. Web directories work well when you're researching a broad area.

In addition to search engines that cover the entire Web, you'll come across more specialised ones that concentrate on particular topics or sites. The technology is the same; they just use a smaller database.

If you're looking for something more specific, you're better off using a search engine. Search engines enable you to search or 'query' a vast database that indexes all the text on millions of Web pages. You type in a few keywords – 'Albert', 'Einstein' and 'relativity', perhaps – and the site returns a list of all the Web pages where they appear. In most cases you get a brief extract that helps you work out which pages are relevant.

Search engines are thorough but not very bright. They'll often return thousands or tens of thousands of 'hits', all of which contain your keywords, but few of which answer your question. If you choose your keywords carefully, though (see page 72), they can be very efficient.

The third type of index is a meta-list – a page of links dedicated to a particular subject, sometimes with brief descriptions of each site. Meta-lists are prepared by people who've spent a lot of time tracking down useful sites and want to share the results.

A search may take you through all three types of index. A Web directory might point you to a meta-list, which might recommend a site, which in turn might have a search engine that helps you find the most relevant page.

Search bar

Internet Explorer's Search bar provides easy access to several search engines. It displays the search controls down the left-hand side of the screen, enabling you to keep the results in view while you check out individual sites.

1 Click the Search button to open the Search bar

2 Tell Internet Explorer what you're trying to find

3 Enter your keywords

4 Click Search

5 A list of pages appears on the left

6 When you click a link, the corresponding Web page is displayed on the right

7 To send the keywords to another search engine, click Next. Click the arrow beside the Next button to select a specific engine

...cont'd

The controls you see when you click the Search button aren't loaded from your hard disk; you're actually looking at a page from Microsoft's Web site. Microsoft sometimes changes this page to add new search engines, so don't be surprised if you open the Search Assistant and find additional choices.

8 Click New when you're ready to start another search

9 The 'Previous searches' option lets you reuse old keywords

10 The 'Find a map' option locates places or landmarks

11 You can also search for files or folders on your computer; computers on your network; or people's e-mail addresses

The Search bar is convenient, but its range of search engines is quite limited and it doesn't tell you how to make the most of them. It's a good idea to visit their Web sites (see pages 78–80 for addresses) to find out about any special facilities they offer.

Customising the Search bar

You'll probably find that some search engines are more helpful than others, and you may not use some of the Search bar's categories. Clear out the dead wood by using the Customize option to fine-tune your choices.

1 Open the Search bar and click the Customize button

If you don't like the Search bar and just want to use your favourite search engine, select 'Use one search service for all searches'. To use the step-by-step searching tool built in to Windows XP, select 'Use Search Companion'.

2 Select the categories and search engines you want to use

3 Move your favourite engine to the top of the list, so it is used first. To do this, select it and click the blue 'Up' button

4 Click Autosearch settings to decide which engine is used for Address bar searches (see the HOT TIP on page 69)

5 Click OK to finish, or Reset to go back to the default settings, or Cancel to go back to Internet Explorer without implementing your changes

6 You may need to close and restart Internet Explorer to see the effect of your changes

Searching tips

Searching the Internet can be frustrating, but with practice it's possible to locate information quickly and efficiently.

Bear the following points in mind:

1   Decide whether you're searching or browsing. If you're looking for general information about a broad topic, such as 'relativity', use a directory to find sites that concentrate on that subject. If you're looking for a specific person or event, use a search engine.

2   Visit the search engine's Home Page, find the instructions and read them. The popular services all have different options, and what works with one won't necessarily work with another. Once you've found an engine you like, stick with it – the others may find a slightly different selection of sites, but you won't miss much.

If you're taken to a long Web page and can't work out where your keywords appear, select Edit>Find or press Ctrl+F to search through the text.

3   Think words, not concepts. Most search engines look for documents containing your keywords, so don't try to describe the concept. You'll get better results by thinking of terms that are likely to appear in the text of a relevant Web page.

4   Refine your search with phrases and extra terms. Most engines allow you to specify that two or more words should appear together, or that the documents must contain some words and not others. For example, searching for 'Einstein' finds over 300,000 pages. Searching for the phrase 'Albert Einstein' brings the total down to 23,000.

5   Use alternatives. Try 'movie' as well as 'film', and don't forget that 'football' is 'soccer' in many parts of the world.

History bar

If there's any chance you might want to return to a page, it's a good idea to make a Favorite or Shortcut for it. However, all isn't lost if you haven't. You can use the History bar to return to pages you've visited in the last couple of weeks.

See page 87 to find out more about the BBC Web site.

1 Click the History button to open the History bar

2 Click the correct day, then find the server where the page resides

Use the mouse to point to one of the listed pages, without clicking. You'll get a pop-up label showing the full name and address.

3 When you find the page you want to return to, click the title to load it into the main window

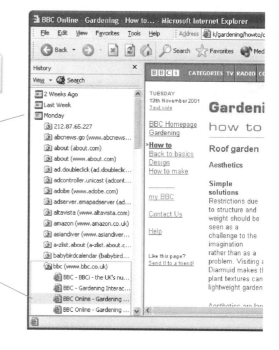

4 If you can't find the page you want to see, click the View button to sort the History bar another way

5 Select By Site if you know where a page was, but can't remember when you last visited it

6 Or, use By Most Visited to bring your favourite sites to the top of the list

7 Or, use By Order Visited Today to review today's browsing

Searching your History

You can hunt through your History for sites that cover a particular subject.

1 Click Search

2 Enter your keyword

3 Click Search Now

4 Relevant pages are listed on the left. Click one to display it on the right

Changing the storage period

You can specify how long the records should be kept. You might want to increase the storage period if you don't log on very often.

1 Go to Tools>Internet Options. Click the General tab

2 Use the Up/Down arrows to adjust the number of days information remains in the History folder

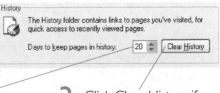

3 Click Clear History if you want to delete your records and start afresh

4 Click OK to finish

Exploring the Web

The Internet has so much to offer that it's hard to know where to start. The best way to learn about the Web is by exploring it, so here's a selection of useful, interesting and entertaining sites that provide a good introduction.

Covers

Chapter Five

Microsoft

Microsoft

`http://www.microsoft.com/`

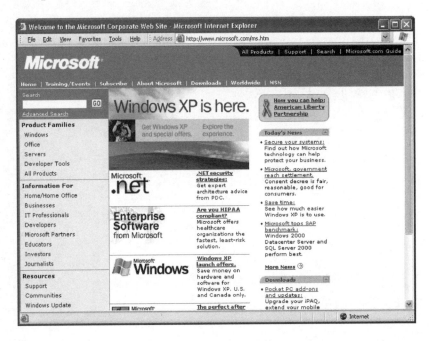

Microsoft's Web site has lots of information about the company's products, including Windows, Word, Excel, Encarta and, of course, Internet Explorer. You can download demos and add-ons, learn about new technologies or use the 'Support' section to solve technical problems. The Knowledge Base – a database of solutions and step-by-step guides used by Microsoft's technical-support people – is worth a look if one of your applications is playing up.

A 'mirror' is a copy of a Web site on another server, often in a different part of the world.

There's also a European mirror of Microsoft's site. It isn't as busy as the main site, so pages and files download quickly. Find it at: `http://www.eu.microsoft.com/`

There's a UK-specific site at: `http://www.microsoft.com/uk/`

The Internet

CNET

`http://www.cnet.com/`

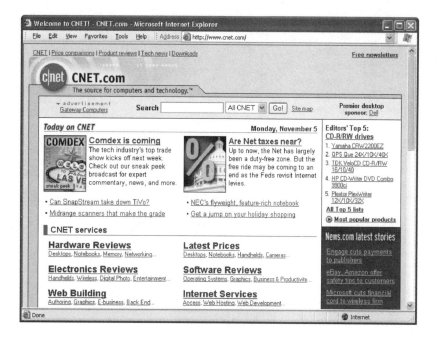

CNET is a vast American Web site covering computers, the Internet and consumer electronics. It offers a mixture of news, reviews and features, plus software to download. Sometimes it seems too big for its own good, but if you click around you'll discover plenty of beginner-friendly items, including 'how to' guides and backgrounders that help you make sense of new technologies.

You could also try:

WiredNews, an electronic spin-off of US Internet magazine *Wired*, for another dose of news and culture. Find it at:
`http://www.wired.com/`

For a UK perspective, try the on-line versions of computer magazines *.net* and *Internet Magazine*:
`http://www.netmag.co.uk/`
`http://www.internet-magazine.com/`

Directories

Yahoo!
`http://www.yahoo.com/`

Most of the sites featured in this chapter are large, well established and unlikely to move or vanish. If you do find that one of the addresses is no longer valid, you may still be able to find the site using a directory or search engine.

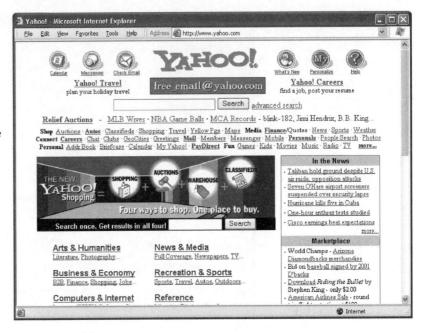

Yahoo! is a hierarchical directory of Web sites and (some) other Internet resources. Each of the 14 categories is progressively subdivided into more tightly defined subcategories, enabling you to work your way down to a list of sites that concentrate on the subject of interest.

For further coverage of Internet sites of interest, see '5000 Brilliant Websites in easy steps pocket'. Find out more about it from the Computer Step site – see page 104.

Yahoo! has several more specialised offshoots, including Yahooligans! for younger browsers, Yahoo! UK & Ireland and the customisable My Yahoo!

You could also try:

About, which employs human guides to catalogue the best sites on over 700 subjects. Find it at:
`http://www.about.com/`

UK Plus, a family-friendly Web directory "dedicated to finding and reviewing everything that a UK reader might consider worth seeing on the Internet". Find it at:
`http://www.ukplus.co.uk/`

Search engines

Google
`http://www.google.com/`

Search engines and directories are some of the most popular sites on the Web. Many offer additional services and there's a lot of overlap between the two types.

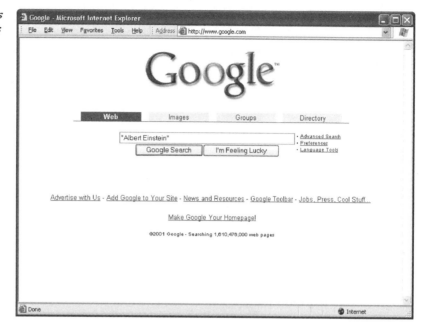

Google is a powerful and popular search engine with a simple interface that makes searching easy. Type in your keywords, click the Google Search button and check out the results. If a page has moved or is inaccessible, you can view an archived version from Google's servers. For tightly targetted searches, click the 'Advanced Search' link and fill in additional details such as the language or file format. Google also enables you to find images and messages posted to Usenet newsgroups (see overleaf).

You could also try:
AltaVista and AltaVista UK for Web sites, images, audio/video files and news items. The main site covers the entire world, whereas the UK version concentrates on local sites. Find them at:
`http://www.altavista.com/`
`http://uk.altavista.com/`

Ask Jeeves, which accepts plain-English questions, at:
`http://www.askjeeves.com/`

Specialised search engines

Yahoo! People Search

`http://people.yahoo.com/`

Forgotten someone's e-mail address? Type their name into Yahoo!'s People Search and it may turn up their details. If you want to make it easier for people to contact you, add your own listing to the directory.

You could also try:

Google Groups, which indexes messages posted to Usenet newsgroups (see Chapter 9), at:
`http://groups.google.com/`

CNET's Search.com enables you to access over 800 specialist search engines. Find it at:
`http://www.search.com/`

Best and worst

Netsurfer Digest
`http://www.netsurf.com/nsd/`

Netsurfer Digest is a weekly newsletter that highlights topical and interesting Web sites. If you find you're clicking around the same old sites, week after week, it'll help you expand your horizons. Read the latest issue (and back issues) on the Web site, or sign up to receive it by e-mail. Additional newsletters focus on science, education and books.

You could also try:
The International Academy of Digital Arts and Sciences dishes out 'Webbies' to the top sites in around 30 categories. Get the details of this year's winners from The Webby Awards, at:
`http://www.webbyawards.com/`

Coolstop, for the best non-commercial sites, at:
`http://coolstop.com/`

The Useless Pages, for a selection of completely pointless (but entertaining) Web sites, at:
`http://www.go2net.com/internet/useless/`

Service providers

Internet Magazine

`http://www.internet-magazine.com/isp/`

Internet Magazine maintains a database of Internet service providers, with details of their offerings and links to their Web sites. You can find a service by name or search for services with particular features.

You could also try:

Easy as 1-2-Free catalogues service providers that don't charge a monthly subscription. Find it at:
`http://www.12free.co.uk/`

The Cybercafe Search Engine lists cyber cafés and public Internet access points in over 150 countries. Find it at:
`http://www.cybercaptive.com/`

Don't forget to visit your service provider's Web site, which may provide technical support as well as details of its services. The information you were sent when you opened your account should include the site's address.

News

Telegraph.co.uk

http://www.telegraph.co.uk/

The on-line edition of *The Telegraph* has everything you'd expect in a printed newspaper, including UK, international and City news, sport, weather, a crossword, cartoons and classified ads. Catch up on older stories by searching the archive, which goes back to November 1994.

You could also try:

BBC News, a typically polished effort with all the headlines plus audio and video, background articles and 'Talking Point' areas where you can vote on topical issues. Find it at:
http://news.bbc.co.uk/

Ananova, a virtual newscaster with green hair. She reads out the headlines on demand at:
http://www.ananova.com/

NewsNow, for links to the top stories from over 100 other news services, sorted by country and category. Find it at:
http://www.newsnow.co.uk/

CNN Interactive

`http://www.cnn.com/`

One of the great things about the Internet is the tremendous choice of viewpoints. As well as browsing British news sites, you can pop over to the United States for an American perspective on US and world news.

CNN's site provides a wide range of clearly presented stories, complete with sound samples and video clips. It's updated throughout the day and there are lots of cross-references and links to other sites.

You could also try:

The New York Times, for in-depth coverage of international and US news. Find it at:
`http://www.nyt.com/`

Kidon Media-Link, for links to on-line news services from all around the globe, at:
`http://www.kidon.com/media-link/`

Weather

The BBC Weather Centre
http://www.bbc.co.uk/weather/

Come rain or shine, the BBC Weather Centre brings you forecasts, weather lore and information about its services. You can meet the team and find out how they produce around 100 forecasts every weekday, or see how this year's weather is measuring up. Other features include a glossary, a temperature convertor, instructions for setting up your own weather station and weather-related games.

You could also try:

The Met Office, for national, regional and marine forecasts and information about weather forecasting, at:
http://www.meto.gov.uk/

Weather.com, the Web site of The Weather Channel, for forecasts for cities all around the world. Find it at:
http://www.weather.com/

Entertainment: Movies

The Internet Movie Database
`http://uk.imdb.com/`

The Internet Movie Database contains everything you're likely to want to know about over 250,000 movies. As well as cast lists, synopses, reviews, trailers, photos and trivia, it has links to official studio sites and fan pages for directors and actors.

You could also try:

Empire Online, the electronic version of the UK film magazine, at: `http://www.empireonline.co.uk/`

Most major releases have promotional Web sites with pictures, sound and video clips, games and so on. Use the Internet Movie Database to track them down.

Television

BBC Online

`http://www.bbc.co.uk/`

BBC Online is the BBC's public-service offering. In addition to news (see page 83) and weather (see page 85), it has information about everything from *TeleTubbies* and *Blue Peter* to *EastEnders*, *Tomorrow's World* and *Watchdog*. You can also check television and radio schedules and get tickets for BBC shows.

You could also try:

Channel 4, for listings and information, at:
`http://www.channel4.com/`

Sky Online, for all things satellite-related, at:
`http://www.sky.co.uk/`

myDigiGuide, for personalised TV and radio listings, at:
`http://www.mydigiguide.com/`

Music

dotmusic

`http://www.dotmusic.com/`

dotmusic is a UK e-zine (electronic magazine) with news, general and specialist charts, and information about many popular artists. You can listen to some of the top tracks and the 'Previews' section has clips of forthcoming singles.

You could also try:

The Ultimate Band List, for information on over 100,000 artists and links to relevant Web sites. Find it at:
`http://ubl.artistdirect.com/`

Jazz Online, which covers all styles of jazz music, "from traditional to straight-ahead to progressive to fusion to contemporary and more". Find it at:
`http://www.jazzonline.com/`

Classical.net, for information about composers, performers, recordings, genres and historical periods, at:
`http://www.classical.net/`

Magazines

National Geographic

http://www.nationalgeographic.com/

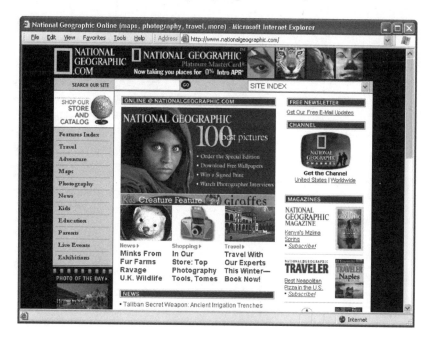

National Geographic has a fabulous Web site, packed with photographs, maps, videos and interactive features. It isn't quite as convenient as the paper version – you can't read it on the train – but it's a lot more exciting. You can also go back to features from the last four or five years – something that isn't always easy with printed magazines.

You could also try:

Time, for political, business and entertainment news, at:
http://www.time.com/

The Economist, for all things financial, at:
http://www.economist.com/

Condé Nast London, for the on-line versions of *Vogue, GQ, Tatler, Vanity Fair, House and Garden, World of Interiors* and *Condé Nast Traveller*, at:
http://www.condenast.co.uk/

E-zines

Salon
`http://www.salon.com/`

The ease and speed with which Web pages can be created has also spawned a host of Web-only magazines or 'e-zines'.

Salon covers arts and entertainment, books, parenting, health, travel and technology. In addition to Sunday supplement-style features, it has interviews, news and media commentary, comic strips and 'table talk' forums. Salon concentrates on quality writing and is updated daily.

You could also try:
Slate, for news, politics and culture, at:
`http://slate.msn.com/`

The Onion, a satirical newspaper for over 18s, at:
`http://www.theonion.com/`

Sport

Football365

`http://www.football365.com/`

Football365 is a football site that's updated 365 days a year – hence the name. Its main attraction is a daily newspaper that is delivered by e-mail. The Web site also has live scores from the English and Scottish leagues, breaking news, discussion forums and humour.

You could also try:

CricInfo, "the home of cricket on the Internet". It's maintained by enthusiasts and has more statistics than you can shake a bat at. Find it at:

`http://www-uk.cricket.org/`

Golf.com, an extensive site with news, commentary and advice for those who like a good walk spoiled, at:

`http://www.golf.com/`

Formula1.com, an unofficial Formula 1 site, at:

`http://www.formula1.com/`

NBA.com

`http://www.nba.com/`

Having access to the Internet makes it easy to follow sports that aren't popular in the UK, such as baseball, basketball and American football. You can also get up-to-the-minute results from international events.

The NBA site enhances its news, previews, results and profiles with lots of multimedia extras, including sound samples and videos. You can also e-mail questions to selected players or join on-line chat sessions.

You could also try:

MLB.com, for Major League baseball, at:
`http://www.mlb.com/`

NFL.com, for the National (American) Football League, at:
`http://www.nfl.com/`

NHL.com, for the National (ice) Hockey League, at:
`http://www.nhl.com/`

Shopping

Amazon.co.uk

http://www.amazon.co.uk/

See page 127 for advice about using your credit card to buy goods over the Internet.

Amazon is one of the most popular on-line retailers. Its UK branch offers over two million books, CDs, videos, DVDs, software titles and electronic gadgets. When you choose a book or CD, it lists other authors or artists bought by people who bought the item you've selected. Start with something you like and there's a good chance the links will lead you to something equally enjoyable. Many items have also been reviewed by previous customers.

You can also order books and CDs from the US branch (http://www.amazon.com/). They take longer to arrive, but you can purchase titles that aren't available in the UK.

You could also try:

CD Universe, for cut-price CDs, at:
http://www.cduniverse.com/

BlackStar, for videos and DVDs, at:
http://www.blackstar.co.uk/

Tesco

http://www.tesco.com/

Books, CDs and videos will keep the family entertained, but sooner or later they'll get hungry. Save yourself the hassle of driving to the supermarket with Tesco's on-line store, which lets you pick out your groceries from an on-line catalogue, then have them delivered to your door. Check the Web site to find out if your area is covered.

You could also try:

Sainsbury's to You, which also delivers in some areas, at http://www.sainsburystoyou.co.uk/

Iceland, which offers nationwide delivery, at:
http://www.iceland.co.uk/

For details of many other on-line shops, including speciality food shops, visit 2020Shops, an on-line directory aimed at UK shoppers. Find it at:
http://www.2020shops.com/

Travel

World Travel Guide

`http://www.travel-guides.com/`

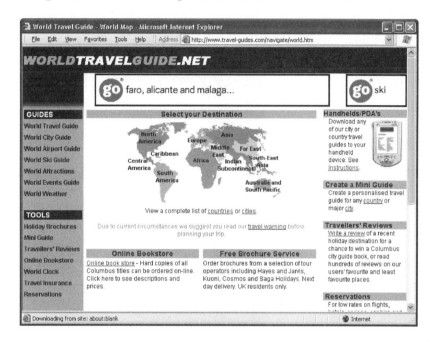

An Internet version of the print publication often used by travel agents, the World Travel Guide is an encyclopædic reference work covering every country in the world (including Antarctica). It's short on atmosphere but long on facts, with information about accommodation, climate, essential documents and contact addresses as well as a general overview for each country.

You could also try:

Expedia, Microsoft's travel-booking site, at:
`http://www.expedia.co.uk/`

Lonely Planet On-line, for independent travellers, at:
`http://www.lonelyplanet.com/`

GORP, the Great Outdoor Recreation Pages, for active holidays with plenty of fresh air and exercise. Find it at:
`http://www.gorp.com/`

Visit Britain

`http://www.visitbritain.com/`

Find out what's worth seeing in the UK with Visit Britain, the British Tourist Authority's Web site. It's relentlessly glowing, but does admit that you might need a waterproof. You can search for activities, events and places to visit or stay, and there's an excellent section on walking.

You could also try:

The RAC, which has an on-line route finder and will e-mail you details of roadworks and traffic jams. Find it at:
`http://www.rac.co.uk/`

Railtrack, for train times, at:
`http://www.railtrack.co.uk/`

National Express, for bus times and on-line bookings, at:
`http://www.nationalexpress.com/`

Multi Media Mapping, for maps of Great Britain, at:
`http://uk.multimap.com/`

Reference

Encyclopædia Britannica
http://www.britannica.com/

Check your facts by searching the on-line edition of the
Encyclopædia Britannica. This is a great resource – it gives you
access to all of the information in the printed version, without the
effort of turning the pages, and also directs you to relevant Web
sites and on-line articles.

You could also try:
Encarta Online, the Internet version of Microsoft's multimedia
encyclopædia, at:
http://encarta.msn.co.uk/

OneLook Dictionaries, which looks for your word in over 700
general and specialist dictionaries. Find it at:
http://www.onelook.com/

My Virtual Reference Desk, for pointers to thousands of reference
sites, at:
http://www.refdesk.com/

Learn2

`http://www.learn2.com/`

Learn2 started out as a guide to the skills of day-to-day life: building fires, making beds, hosting dinner parties, throwing frisbees. It's now more interested in selling you on-line courses, mostly dealing with computer software, but if you head for the 'Everyday Tutorials' section, you'll find hundreds of '2torials' on everything from arts and crafts to technology.

You could also try:

Delia Online, for recipes and advice from the queen of the boiled egg, Delia Smith. Find it at:
`http://www.deliaonline.com/`

Expertgardener, hosted by the ubiquitous Alan Titchmarsh and Charlie Dimmock, for help with your plants. Find it at:
`http://www.expertgardener.com/`

NHS Direct, for health information, at:
`http://www.nhsdirect.nhs.uk/`

...cont'd

UKonline

http://www.ukonline.gov.uk/

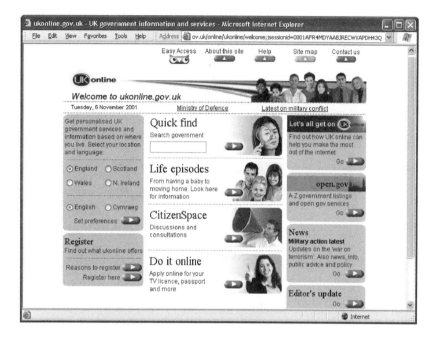

UKonline is a gateway to the multitude of government Web sites. The 'Life episodes' section helps you find information relevant to particular events, such as having a baby or moving home. If you're looking for a specific organisation, go to the 'Quick find' section for A–Z lists. From here you can click through to the Foreign and Commonwealth Office Web site, which has travel advice, or the Inland Revenue Web site, for help with your tax return, and so on. There's also a 'Citizen space' section that explains how to vote and encourages you to contribute to government policy.

You could also try:

Want to know how much it costs to send an airmail letter to New Zealand? Ask Royal Mail, at:
http://www.royalmail.co.uk/

Want to check the price of a phone call? Try BT, at:
http://www.bt.com/

Science

NASA
`http://www.nasa.gov/`

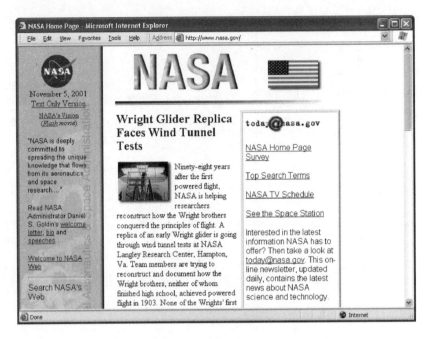

The NASA home page is the gateway to a vast collection of information about space and space exploration. Highlights include day-by-day reports from the shuttle, lots of historical information and a 'today@nasa.gov' section with the latest news. It can be hard to work out where your topic might be covered, but few institutions surpass NASA for quantity or quality of publicly available information.

You could also try:
The Why Files, for "the science behind the news", at:
`http://whyfiles.org/`

Discovery Channel Online, for a wide range of features with lots of pictures and interactive extras, at:
`http://www.discovery.com/`

New Scientist, for news, features, jobs and answers to questions such as, "Why do flying fish fly?" Find it at:
`http://www.newscientist.com/`

Computing: Reference

PC Webopaedia

http://www.pcwebopaedia.com/

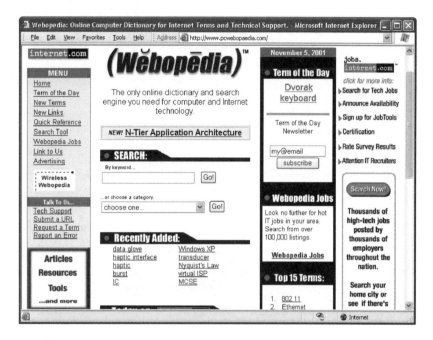

The PC Webopaedia specialises in explaining computer jargon. Search for terms you've encountered in magazines, or browse through the categories to expand your knowledge. You can also look at the top-15 list of most requested terms to find out what's puzzling other Internet users. Many definitions have links to Websites where you can get more in-depth coverage.

You could also try:

Whatis?com, another IT-specific encyclopedia, at:
http://whatis.techtarget.com/

The PC Technology Guide, which explains what the bits and bobs inside (or attached to) your PC actually do, at:
http://www.pctechguide.com/

Maximum PC, for reams of information from computer magazines produced by Future Publishing. Find it at:
http://www.maximumpc.co.uk/

Hardware

Dell
http://www.dell.co.uk/

Most computer manufacturers have extensive sites that showcase their products, provide technical support and even enable you to buy equipment on-line. They often have a lot more information than you'd find in an advertisement or get from a sales assistant.

Dell's Web site is no exception: you can examine typical systems, or design your own and order it on-line. The technical support section has solutions to common problems and you can download the latest driver software.

You could also try:
If you're looking for a new modem, all the manufacturers have Web sites. Try some of the following:

*   3Com/US Robotics, at: http://www.3com.co.uk/

*   Diamond, at: http://www.diamondmm.com/

*   Zoom/Hayes, at: http://www.zoomtel.com/

Software

Adobe

`http://www.adobe.com/`

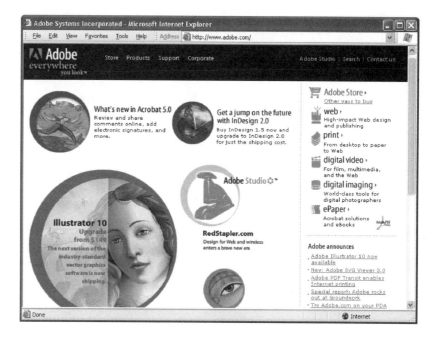

Graphics specialist Adobe has an excellent Web site that provides detailed information about all its products. You can download tryout versions of most programs or get updates and extras for the ones you already own. The 'Support' section has tutorials that help you master new techniques.

You could also try:

Corel, creator of CorelDRAW and Corel WordPerfect, at:
`http://www.corel.com/`

Symantec, for utility and antivirus software, at:
`http://www.symantec.co.uk/`

Use Yahoo! (see page 78) or a search engine to track down other hardware and software companies.

Computer books

Computer Step

`http://www.ineasysteps.com/`

Find out about the other titles in this series from the on-line home of Computer Step, the leading British publisher of computer books.

You could also try:

Computer Manuals, a mail-order business that specialises in computer books, at:
`http://www.compman.co.uk/`

Amazon, an on-line bookshop with lots of information about books and their authors (see page 93). Find it at:
`http://www.amazon.co.uk/`

Extending your browser

This chapter explains how to teach Internet Explorer new tricks. It shows you how to update your software and install ActiveX controls. It also covers the most popular add-ons.

Covers

Chapter Six

Updating your software

Microsoft is constantly refining its Internet software, so the programs on your Windows XP disc may not have all the latest bells and whistles. Visit the Windows Update Web site to download updates that solve problems and add new features.

1 Go to the Start menu and select All Programs>Windows Update. When the Web site is displayed, click the 'Scan for updates' link

Critical updates solve problems that may crash your computer or make it vulnerable to hackers (see pages 120 and 125). You should always download and install them. Optional updates solve minor problems and add features to your software. You may also be able to download entirely new programs that have been developed since Windows XP was released.

2 Windows Update looks at the software installed on your computer and works out what you can add. If there are any critical updates, they are automatically displayed in the right-hand frame.

3 To see any optional updates, click the 'Windows XP' link

4 To select an update, click the Add button immediately beneath it

5 When you've selected everything you want, click the 'Review and install updates' link. Follow the on-screen instructions to download and install your new software

Install on demand

When you install Windows XP, you automatically install Internet Explorer. However, you don't install all the components. Files for some of the less popular features, such as the ability to display Chinese or Japanese characters, aren't copied onto your hard disk. If you come across a Web site that uses these characters, Internet Explorer prompts you to install the missing software.

1. A dialogue box informs you that extra files are required. Click Install to copy them onto your hard disk, or Cancel to carry on regardless

2. If you've opted to install the files, insert your Windows CD and click OK

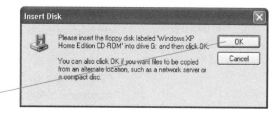

3. The extra files are installed. You should be able to view the Web site straight away, but you may need to restart your computer to get the full benefit

Sony's Japanese Web site is at: `http://www.sony.co.jp/`
For information in English, try: `http://www.sony-europe.com/`

ActiveX Controls

ActiveX Controls are also known as 'plug-ins'. This is a more general term that's used to describe small programs that can be 'plugged in' to bigger ones to add new features.

ActiveX Controls are small pieces of software that add new features to Internet Explorer. They're often used to handle multimedia files, such as new types of sound and video file, animations and 360-degree panoramas.

You can think of ActiveX Controls as the electronic equivalent of extra blades for your food processor. Each time you want to do something new, you download the extra software that enables Internet Explorer to slice, dice, shred and otherwise process the data. Some of these add-ons are produced by Microsoft, but most come from other companies.

Most ActiveX Controls are installed automatically. When you visit a page that requires a new one, Internet Explorer locates and downloads it (see opposite). You get the option to abort the installation, but otherwise everything is done for you. You shouldn't even have to disconnect from the Internet.

Some add-ons have to be installed by hand (see page 110). Once you've checked that the software is compatible with Internet Explorer, download the version for your operating system, then log off and run the setup program.

Despite the confusing terminology, installing add-ons is actually quite straightforward. If you need an ActiveX Control to view a Web page, Internet Explorer should install it for you. If it doesn't, you probably need to install the software yourself, in which case there'll be a link to a site you can download it from.

Automatic installation

Most ActiveX Controls are very easy to install. When you come across a Web page that requires a new one, Internet Explorer downloads it automatically.

1 Internet Explorer displays a security warning (see page 122) and asks if you want to install the ActiveX Control

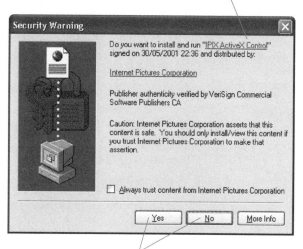

2 Click Yes if you have confidence in the company that published the software, or No to abort the installation

3 If you click Yes, the Control is installed. Internet Explorer is able to make use of it straight away, so you'll see or hear the additional material in a few seconds

Manual installation

If you have to install an add-on by hand, you'll be directed to the home page of the company that supplies it. For example, sites that use RealAudio (see page 112) normally provide a 'Get RealPlayer' button that takes you to the RealNetworks Home Page.

Check the system requirements for an add-on before you download it. Note also that plug-ins that work with older versions of Internet Explorer don't always work with version 6 (the version supplied with Windows XP).

You'll probably need to enter your details in a form. This enables the Web site to give you the correct version

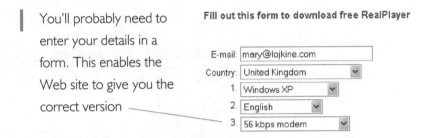

Download the file, just as you would any other program file (see page 45). Make sure you know what it's called and where you've put it

Once you've disconnected from the Internet, locate the file using My Computer or Windows Explorer. Double-click it to start the setup routine and install the add-on

Shockwave and Flash

Shockwave, Flash and RealPlayer (see overleaf) are the 'must-have' add-ons. They enable you to view some of the most exciting sites on the Web, so most people end up installing them.

Shockwave and Flash add visual pizazz to the Web. The Flash player is used to display animations and special effects. Its more sophisticated sibling, the Shockwave player, gives you access to multimedia presentations and games.

Flash animations are very compact, download quickly and can include interactive elements, such as buttons that react when you point or click. They're often used to add movement to the main page of a Web site.

Macromedia's Shockwave site has lots of games and animations and is great fun to explore. Find it at: `http://www.shockwave.com/`

Shockwave movies are more complex and take longer to download. They can combine text, graphics, animation, digital video, sound and interactive elements. You're most likely to find them on entertainment sites.

Both players are produced by Macromedia. Find out more from: `http://www.macromedia.com/`

RealPlayer

See page 44 to find out how streaming works.

RealPlayer is produced by streaming-sound pioneer RealNetworks. It enables you to listen to RealAudio sound and watch RealVideo video, both of which play as they download. There's no waiting around – you start hearing or seeing the clip a few seconds after you click the link.

RealAudio is often used to transmit radio shows, news bulletins and special events over the Internet. Sound quality deteriorates when the Internet is very busy, but generally it's pretty good, especially for voice broadcasts. Music doesn't transmit as well, but you can recognise your favourite songs. Sites that sell CDs often have RealAudio clips of sample tracks so you can check that you're buying the right disk.

RealVideo gives you pictures as well as sound, but doesn't work quite as well over dial-up connections. The pictures are small and fuzzy and it can be hard to work out what's going on. However, there's something exciting about using the Internet to tune into a television signal from the other side of the world.

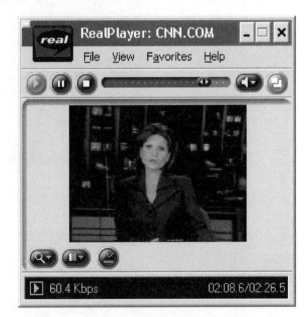

Get RealPlayer from the RealNetworks Web site at:
`http://www.real.com/`

Use the Channels and Radio menus to find something to watch or listen to, or visit the RealGuide Web site for details of special broadcasts. Find it at:
`http://realguide.real.com/`

QuickTime

The QuickTime player enables you to play video clips recorded in Apple's QuickTime format. It can also handle video, sound and image files saved in many other formats.

QuickTime movies may play in a separate window or be integrated into the Web page – it depends on the Web designer's wishes.

There's a lot of overlap between Windows Media Player (supplied with Windows), RealPlayer and the QuickTime player. They all play most types of video clip and they all support streaming. However, some clips only play in the 'correct' player, so you'll probably end up with all three on your hard disk.

The main reason for installing the QuickTime player is that the format has become popular for movie trailers. The Apple Web site has a section devoted to QuickTime promos for new films, at: `http://www.apple.com/trailers/`

Other attractions include QuickTime TV, which is used for Internet broadcasts, and QuickTime VR (Virtual Reality). QuickTime VR files are similar to IPIX images (see overleaf).

Download the QuickTime player from: `http://www.apple.com/quicktime/`

IPIX

The IPIX viewer, produced by Interactive Pictures Corporation, enables you to step inside 360-by-360-degree panoramic images. It creates the illusion that you are standing in the middle of a scene, able to spin round and look in any direction. You can also zoom in or out, and sometimes there are clickable 'hotspots' that take you on to other images. IPIX images are used to show you the interiors of houses, hotels and museums, and to take you to places you're unlikely to visit personally, such as the International Space Station.

Find out more from the IPIX Home Page at:
http://www.ipix.com/

Use the IPIX viewer to explore sets from popular police drama The Bill at: http://www.thebill.com/

There are several other formats for panoramic images. The one you're most likely to encounter is QuickTime VR, which requires Apple's QuickTime movie player (see previous page).

Acrobat

Adobe's Acrobat Reader is a page-viewing tool that enables you to browse documents saved as PDF (Portable Document Format) files. This format preserves the layout of a document as well as its content, so the copy you see on your screen looks the same as a printed copy of the original file. You can't edit the PDF version, but you can read or print it – even if you don't have the DTP program or word processor used to create the document.

PDF files are used to distribute electronic versions of brochures and forms. They look good and print out well, so they're a popular choice when presentation is important. They also make it easy for companies to put existing documents on the Web.

Once you've installed Acrobat Reader, PDF files can be viewed from within Internet Explorer. The two programs work together, displaying both sets of tools in the same window. This means you can jump from a Web page to a PDF file, or vice versa, without switching applications.

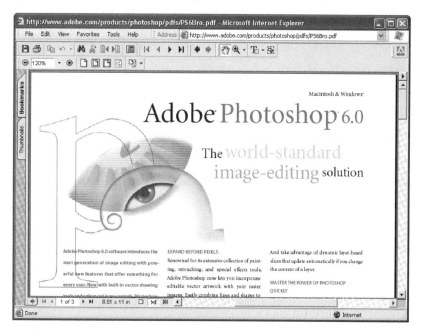

Find out more from Adobe's Web site at:
`http://www.adobe.com/`

Menus, buttons and bars

You can also install add-ons that give you new toolbars, buttons, menu options or Explorer bars. As with ActiveX controls, some of these add-ons come from Microsoft, but most are developed by other companies.

The fact that service providers and software developers can extend and customise Internet Explorer is one of the reasons for its popularity. However, it does mean other people's copies may not be exactly the same as yours. If you come across a copy that has extra features, don't assume your version is 'broken'. You just don't have the same add-ons as your friend.

Google toolbar

The Google search engine (see page 79) offers a toolbar that makes it easy to search the Web. You can also search individual Web sites, which is handy when you're trying to find something on a site that doesn't have its own search engine.

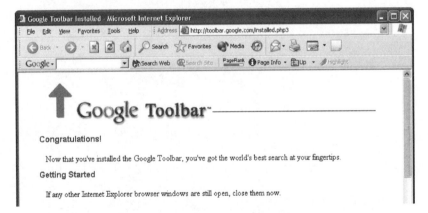

Installing the toolbar is much like installing an ActiveX control (see page 109). Simply follow the on-screen instructions and click Yes when the security warning appears.

Once you've installed it, the toolbar can be moved around and turned on or off in the usual way (see page 25)

AI Roboform

Roboform is form-filling utility created by Siber Systems (the 'AI' stands for 'Artificial Intelligence'). Once you've told it personal details such as your name and address, it can fill in forms on your behalf. All you have to do is click the Fill Ident button.

For more on AI Roboform, visit the Siber Systems Web site, at:
http://www.siber.com/roboform/

AI Roboform also adds new options to the Standard buttons, the Tools menu and the menu that appears when you right-click on a Web page. Most of these items can be removed or turned off.

To remove the Roboform software itself (and most other add-ons), click the Start button and select Control Panel. Click Add or Remove programs, select AI Roboform (or the add-on you wish to remove) and click the Change/Remove button

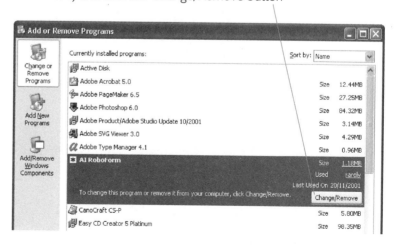

iMarkup Explorer bar

iMarkup from iMarkup Solutions Incorporated is an annotation utility that enables you to attach notes to Web pages. When you return to the page, your note reappears. It's the Internet equivalent of adding sticky notes to a reference book or report.

iMarkup's tools appear in an Explorer bar down the left-hand side of the main window. It also gives you an extra toolbar, a button to add to the Standard Buttons, and some new menu options.

For more information about iMarkup or to download a trial version, visit the site at: http://www.imarkup.com/

Extra toolbar   Extra button

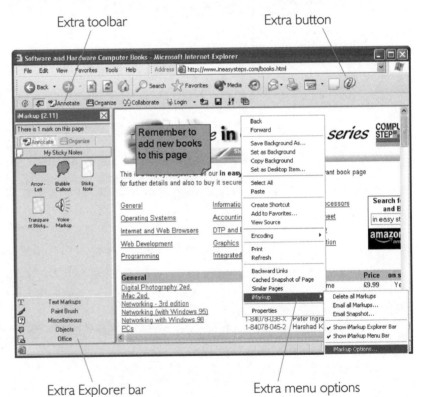

Extra Explorer bar   Extra menu options

You'll see other add-ons mentioned in Internet magazines, or come across them as you browse the Web. You can also visit a search engine (see page 79) and search for 'Explorer bar'.

Internet security

This chapter discusses the vexing questions of Internet security and on-line pornography. You'll learn how to avoid viruses, hackers and scams, protect your privacy and make the Internet safe for children.

Covers

Chapter Seven

Security

When you connect your computer to the Internet, you're able to access a great wealth of information. Unfortunately, you also expose your own data to hackers and viruses.

The prospect of losing important information makes many people dubious about purchasing a modem. In reality, your files are more likely to be destroyed by errors and hardware failures, and you probably do a dozen potentially unsafe things every day. There are risks associated with using the Internet, and it's a good idea to be aware of them, but it isn't difficult to keep them at a manageable level. Internet Explorer's Security zones (see page 125) make it easy to select sensible security settings for several types of Web site.

If you use your computer to store information that is confidential, irreplaceable or valuable to others, consult a security expert before connecting it to the Internet. On the other hand, if losing the data on your hard disk would merely be irritating and inconvenient, you can protect yourself against most types of attack by making regular backups of important files. In either case, following the advice given over the next few pages will reduce the chances of anything going wrong.

Viruses

There are several types of malicious program, including viruses, worms and Trojan horses. A virus attaches itself to other programs. A worm can replicate independently and doesn't need to attach itself to a program. Trojans don't replicate – they just cause damage if you make the mistake of running them.

A computer virus is a small piece of program code that attaches itself to other programs. When you run the infected program, the virus copies itself to another program or causes your computer to do something untoward. Some are just irritating, but others may damage or destroy your files.

You can only 'catch' a computer virus by running an infected program. As well as checking all the software you download, you should be wary of programs attached to e-mails and newsgroup messages. If you aren't sure how to identify program files (it gets harder every year), be suspicious of anything sent to you by a stranger. You can't trust your friends, either. If you get a message that seems out of character, don't open any attached files. Check with the friend first – the message may have been sent without their knowledge.

Software that is incomplete, badly written or simply incompatible with one of your other applications can also upset your computer. The more you download, the more important it is to make backups.

Protect yourself by investing in antivirus software and updating it regularly. It's also a good idea to establish a schedule for backing up files that contain important information or would be difficult to replace. Download software from large, well-managed file archives or directly from the company concerned.

Macro viruses

Files that may contain macros, such as Microsoft Word and Excel documents, can also carry viruses. Macro viruses are a particularly sneaky development, because the files they infect don't look like programs. They've become very common in recent years and even documents from reputable sources may be infected.

To find out how to avoid macro viruses in your version of Word or Excel, consult the Help file. The procedure depends on the version.

Recent versions of Word and Excel can protect you against macro viruses. If you're using a very old version that doesn't have this option, use a virus checker on any Word or Excel files before you open them.

Authenticode

It's impossible to make the most of the Web without downloading lots of add-ons (see Chapter 6). However, it's difficult to be sure whether you're downloading a useful utility that will enhance your Web browsing or a rogue program designed to attack your system. There's also the risk that a genuine program might have been sabotaged somewhere along its journey.

To counter these fears, Microsoft has developed a system called Authenticode that helps you decide whether you can safely install an add-on. It enables publishers to add a 'digital signature' to their software, so you can be sure of its origin. These signatures are the on-line equivalent of the holograms attached to Microsoft's software boxes – they demonstrate that the application is genuine.

The digital signature takes the form of a certificate that verifies the identity of the publisher of the program. The presence of a certificate also proves that the program hasn't been tampered with along the way.

Authenticode works for programs that are installed from within Internet Explorer. If you save an installation file on to your hard disk instead of selecting Open to run it straight away, you won't see the certificate.

1 When you download an upgrade or add-on, you'll be shown its certificate. If it's unsigned, you'll get a warning message instead

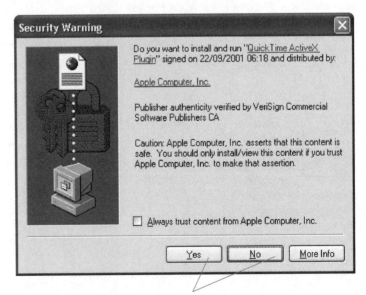

2 Click Yes to continue the installation or No if you don't have confidence in the publisher

Virus hoaxes

There are a number of virus hoaxes that do the rounds by e-mail. The best-known example is a message that tells you not to open messages with 'Good Times' in the subject line. Doing so will delete your files and destroy your processor – or so the story goes.

This is nonsense, because you cannot catch a virus from a text-only e-mail message. However, the Good Times hoax is almost as troublesome as a real virus, because people waste a lot of time sending the message to their friends, calling their systems manager and so on.

If you receive a warning that you think might be a hoax, don't pass it on 'just in case'. You'll get your less knowledgeable friends worried over nothing, and those with more experience will think you're gullible.

How can you tell whether a virus warning is a hoax? You should be suspicious of any warning message that:

1   Contains lots of exclamation marks!!!!!

2   Tells you something dreadful will happen if you open an e-mail message with a particular title.

3   Promises total destruction of your hard disk, your processor, your entire computer, your home…

4   References a technical-sounding organisation you've never heard of and can't find on the Web.

5   Encourages you to pass it on to all your friends.

You can find out whether your message is a well-known hoax by looking it up on one of the following Web sites:

CIAC Internet Hoaxes, at:
`http://hoaxbusters.ciac.org/`

Symantec's Anti-virus Resource Center, at:
`http://www.symantec.com/avcenter/`

Chain letters and scams

It's an unfortunate fact of Internet life that the ease with which you can send e-mail or create Web pages encourages some people to abuse these services. You shouldn't believe everything you read on the Web and you shouldn't take every e-mail message seriously.

Chain letters

There are two sorts of chain letter. One type has a list of names and promises you enormous wealth if you send a small sum of money to the person at the top. You're then supposed to add your name and redistribute the message. It's mathematically impossible for most of these schemes to pay off, and they're probably illegal. Many service providers will close your account if they catch you forwarding this kind of junk.

The other type promises you good luck if you forward it to all your friends, and bad luck if you don't. Some of these messages are very unpleasant and you should delete them. You are not doing your friends any favours by sending them messages that threaten all sorts of dire consequences if they 'break the chain'.

The Craig Shergold story is an urban legend – a tale that keeps being told, regardless of its veracity. You can find many more in The AFU & Urban Legends Archive, at: `http://www.urbanlegends.com/`

There are also some well-meaning chain letters that ask you to send cards to a sick child – usually Craig Shergold, a boy with cancer – who is trying to get into *The Guinness Book of Records*. There's actually some truth to this story, which dates back to the late 1980s. However, Shergold got his record, had an operation and got on with his life, so there's no need to send a card. The organisations mentioned in the letter receive quite enough unwanted mail already.

Scams

There are numerous scams circulating the Internet, some of which are quite convincing. Be suspicious of anything that sounds too good to be true, and learn to recognise the most common tricks.

Internet ScamBusters is a good source of information and advice, and issues regular newsletters. Find it at: `http://www.scambusters.org/`

Other hazards

If someone reports a serious weakness in Internet Explorer, Microsoft releases a 'patch' – a small upgrade that fixes the problem. Get the latest ones from its Web site, at: `http:// www.microsoft.com/ windows/ie/download/ default.asp`

Almost all the things that make Web sites interesting can also be abused to cause you problems. Scripts and ActiveX Controls can potentially be used to attack your computer, although so far the risks seem more theoretical than actual. People keep discovering different ways these technologies can be used to steal passwords or monitor your browsing, but the reports are coming from researchers rather than victims.

Trying to make an accurate assessment of the risks to your computer will give you a headache. Most on-line activities are potentially dangerous, but then so are most kitchen implements. The problem is compounded by the fact that your confidence will vary from site to site. You probably trust well-known companies to produce 'safe' Web sites, but you might have a few qualms about the skills and intentions of a complete unknown.

Internet Explorer's warnings are just that – warnings. It isn't telling you that what you want to do will cause a problem, just that it might. It's up to you to decide whether there's genuine cause for concern.

To make things simpler, Internet Explorer provides four security settings – High, Medium, Medium-Low and Low. These settings cover all kinds of interactive content, plus file downloads and communication with insecure sites (see page 127). The High setting prevents you from downloading anything that could cause problems, keeping you safe but cutting you off from some of the more exciting aspects of the Web. Medium is less severe: it bans some unsafe content and warns you about the rest. Medium-Low is the same, but without the warnings. It's a rejigged Medium setting for people who always ignore the warning messages. Finally, the Low setting enables anyone and everyone to mess with your computer.

Rather than making you use the same setting for every site you visit, Internet Explorer divides the Internet into four 'zones': Local Intranet (your company's internal network), Trusted, Internet and Restricted. Initially all Web sites are in the Local Intranet or Internet zones (if you connect with a modem, they'll all be in the Internet zone). As you gain experience, you can add sites to the Trusted ('safe') and Restricted ('unsafe') zones. Internet Explorer will be more lenient or more protective when you visit those sites.

It only takes a couple of minutes to decide what level of protection you require and select a security setting. You can then let Internet Explorer do the worrying and get on with browsing the Web.

1 To choose a security setting, go to Tools > Internet Options, then click the Security tab

2 Choose the Internet zone

If you're a security expert, you can fine-tune your security setting by clicking Custom. This option enables you to select the types of content you want to allow and avoid.

3 Move the slider to High (at the top) to eliminate potential hazards

4 Medium security exposes you to some risks, but enables you to enjoy interactive Web content. You receive warnings about potential hazards. Medium-Low is the same, but without the warning messages

5 Low security is only recommended for sites on your (adequately protected) company network

If you're using Internet Explorer at work, your systems manager may have added some sites to the Trusted and Restricted zones. If not, it's up to you to decide which sites fall in these categories.

1 To add a site to the Trusted or Restricted zone, click the appropriate icon, then click Sites. Enter the address and click Add. Click OK to finish

On-line shopping

As well as protecting the data on your computer, you need to think about the information you transmit over the Internet. You probably don't care whether the keywords you submit to search engines can be intercepted (and it's unlikely a hacker would bother), but you won't want to share your credit-card number with other Internet users.

Do not enter your credit-card number into insecure forms or include it in e-mail messages. The same rules apply to any other confidential information.

Internet shopping is fairly safe as long as you stick to reputable companies that use secure servers to collect your details. When you're connected to a secure server, all the data you send is encrypted to protect it from eavesdroppers. There are several ways to identify a secure server:

1 Internet Explorer informs you that you're opening a secure connection

2 Secure Web addresses begin with `https://` rather than the usual `http://`

3 A padlock icon 🔒 appears at the right-hand end of the Status bar

If a Web site uses frames (see page 52), it's hard to tell whether it is secure. Right-click within the frame that holds the order form and select Properties to check the status of the connection.

4 Double-click the padlock to see the site's security certificate

5 Internet Explorer displays another warning when you leave the secure server

You may have to pay duty and VAT on items bought from overseas Web sites. The Customs and Excise publication 'Notice 143: A Guide for International Post Users' explains the rules. Find it on the Customs and Excise Web site at: `http://www.hmce.gov.uk/`

You can also protect yourself by sticking to a few simple rules when you're shopping on-line.

1   Give your money to companies you're familiar with, or whose sites have been recommended by people you trust.

2   Look around before you buy. Can you find the company's street address and phone number? How much will delivery cost? Will the company take your goods back if there's a problem? Good shopping sites provide plenty of information about their services.

3   If you aren't sure about a company, request a catalogue or make contact over the phone.

4   Pay by credit card and use UK-based shops where possible. You have more protection under these circumstances.

5   Print out details of your order (see page 55), and keep any confirmation e-mails you receive.

6   Check your credit-card statement each month and make sure you can account for all the purchases.

7   Choose a different password for each shopping site, and keep these passwords secret. Many sites keep a record of your details, which is very convenient if you make regular purchases. However, it enables anyone who knows your password to enjoy an afternoon's shopping at your expense (see opposite for more on passwords).

Internet shopping can save you time and money and enable you to buy things you wouldn't normally get in the shops. Don't be put off by all these warnings – if you shop sensibly, it may be safer than walking down the street with a bulging wallet in your back pocket.

Passwords

Passwords are the bane of Internet users' lives. If you aren't thinking one up for a site you've just discovered, you're trying to recall the one you chose last week.

Choosing passwords

There are two common ways for someone to break your password: they can guess it, or they can use a program that works through a dictionary, trying every word. Try to choose passwords that are immune to both types of attack. Don't use your name, your partner's name, your date of birth or any other easily obtainable information. Where possible, choose a mixture of numbers and letters, and make each password at least six characters long.

Remembering passwords

Never reveal the password that you use to connect to the Net to anyone you meet on-line, even if they claim that they work for your service provider and need your details to prevent a problem with your account. Anyone who asks for this information is up to no good.

If you log on to the Internet from home and lead a fairly blameless life, choosing good passwords is less important than finding some way to remember the ones you've already picked.

Internet Explorer can remember many passwords for you. It doesn't do this by default; instead, it asks if you want this feature turned on the first time you type a password into a Web site. If you click Yes, it will offer to remember each password you enter.

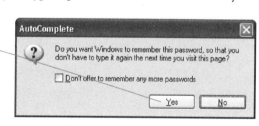

You may want to use this feature for sites where your password simply gives you access. It's less of a good thing on shopping sites, where it may enable family members to access your account and make purchases with your credit card.

> To turn this feature off, go to Tools>Internet Options. Click the Content tab, then click the AutoComplete button. Deselect the 'User names and passwords' option. You can also clear the password list

.NET Passport

To find out more, visit the .NET Passport Web site, at: http://www.passport.com/

.NET Passport is a centralised password service run by Microsoft. Once you have a Passport, you can use your e-mail address and Passport password to log in to any Web site that uses this technology. You can also create a Passport wallet that stores your credit-card details, enabling you to check out more quickly at participating on-line stores.

Think twice about creating a Passport wallet. This service is new, and as yet unproven. Most of the sites that use it are based in the US, so you won't have many chances to use your wallet.

The advantage of the Passport system is that you only have one password to remember. The disadvantage is that if someone else discovers that password, they can pretend to be you on a number of sites. If you've created a wallet, they can spend your money.

You'll be prompted to create a Passport when you try to access Microsoft services such as Hotmail (see page 160) and Windows Messenger (see Chapter 10). Alternatively, you can sign up from the User Accounts section of Control Panel.

1 Click the Start button and select Control Panel, then click User Accounts. If several accounts are listed, select your own. Click 'Set up my account to use a .NET password' to activate the .NET Passport Wizard

2 Click Next to continue (and after each step)

3 When you're asked if you have an e-mail address, click Yes

If you have an e-mail account with Hotmail or MSN.com, you already have a Passport. Enter the address and corresponding password to add the Passport to your Windows XP user account.

4 Enter your e-mail address

5 Think up a password and enter it twice

...cont'd

The secret question and location details helps you confirm your identity if you forget your password and need to choose a new one.

6 Choose one of the secret questions and enter the answer

7 Fill in your country, region and postcode

8 Read the Terms of Use and select 'I accept the agreement' if you're happy with them

If you decide to share your information, you won't need to re-enter your details when you register with Passport-enabled sites (see DON'T FORGET, below). To change these settings, go to the Passport Web site and select 'Member Services'.

9 Decide which details you want to share with sites that you log on to using Passport

10 You're done. Click Finish to close the wizard

Your .NET Passport can be used on any Passport-enabled site.

1 Look for a Sign In button near the top of the main page, and click it

The first time you sign in to a site that uses the Passport system, you may be asked to register. This associates additional information with your Passport, for that site only. When you sign in again, your Passport identifies you and enables the site to find the extra details in its database.

2 Check your e-mail address, fill in your password and click OK

3 When you're ready to leave, click the Sign Out button

7. Internet security | 131

Privacy

As you browse the Web, you'll notice that a lot of sites want to know who you are, where you live, how old you are, what sort of music you like, and so on. Sometimes a Web site has a good reason for collecting this data. A weather site needs to know where you are to provide the correct forecast, and an on-line shop needs your address to deliver your goods.

A weather site is just a convenient example. Weather sites are no worse than any other type of Web site.

Sometimes there's another reason for collecting personal data: marketing. If a weather site wants to know what kind of music you listen to, it might be planning to pass on your details to companies that sell CDs or concert tickets. The result is a load of junk mail from companies you've never heard of. You don't recall giving them your details because you didn't – they bought them from the weather site.

Another concern is consolidation of personal information. Suppose one site wants your address, another site asks for your date of birth, and a third one wants your mother's maiden name. If they share their information, they can build up a detailed profile.

Cookies

Some of the information you enter into on-line forms ends up on your hard disk, in a file called a 'cookie'. Here's how it works:

If a Web page includes an advert, the advertiser may also create a cookie on your hard disk. They can use it to keep track of the pages you've visited or the adverts you've seen.

Suppose you visit a weather site and enter your name (John) and postcode (EC1). The site tells your Web browser to record the information in a cookie file, which is stored in your Windows folder. Next time you visit the site, it asks your browser to send back the information from the cookie. It then creates a customised Web page with a personalised message: 'Hello John, it's raining in London, so don't forget your umbrella.'

The advantage of this system is that you get the forecast you want, straight away. The disadvantage is that the site knows who you are. If you start checking the weather in Spain or Greece, it might give your e-mail address to a travel agent.

Reputable sites have privacy statements that explain what they do with the information they collect. Once you've read the statement, you can decide whether to enter your details.

Privacy settings

Reading privacy statements is tedious, so Internet Explorer gives you an alternative. It can accept or reject cookies automatically, based on your predefined preferences.

The privacy features rely on a new system developed by the Platform for Privacy Preferences Project (P3P). It enables Web sites to convert their privacy statements into a standard, computer-readable format. When you visit a Web site, Internet Explorer reads its privacy statement, compares it to your settings and treats cookies accordingly.

The Platform for Privacy Preferences Project (P3P) was developed by the World Wide Web Consortium (W3C), which oversees the Web. Find out more about it from the W3C Web site, at: http://www.w3.org/P3P/

1 To enter your preferences, go to Tools>Internet Options. Click the Privacy tab

2 Move the slider to select a privacy setting. Higher settings reduce the amount of data collected, but may mean Web sites can't offer you personalised services

3 If you want to use a different setting for a particular site, click the Edit button and enter its address

4 Click OK

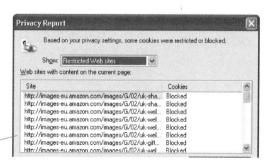

P3P is a new standard, so many sites haven't yet computerised their privacy statements. It'll be a while before everything works exactly as it ought.

5 When Internet Explorer rejects a cookie, you'll see a privacy icon in the status bar. Double-click it for a report

Pornography

Talk to someone who has never used the Internet and they will almost certainly ask you about pornography. They might not know what the Internet is or how it works, but reading the papers has given them the impression that every other Web page contains X-rated material – or worse.

Most adult sites have no desire to provide pornographic material to children. They usually have warnings on the front page and many require credit-card details as part of the registration process.

Truthfully, there is a lot of adult material on the Internet. Most of it is perfectly legal, although not to everyone's taste; some of it is deeply unpleasant and definitely illegal in this country. The global nature of the Internet, combined with the speed at which sites come and go, makes it almost impossible to eradicate illegal images. As for the rest, the problem is not so much that it is there, but that anyone can access it – including children.

If you have a family, you are probably concerned about the sort of material your children might encounter. At the same time, there are many excellent, child-friendly Web sites. Preventing your children from accessing the Internet may protect them from inappropriate material, but it also cuts them off from all kinds of useful information.

There's no easy way to have the 'good' bits of the Internet without also enabling a computer-savvy child to find some of the 'bad' bits. However, there are several things you can do to minimise the risks. First, install the computer in a family room, so you can keep an eye on the screen, and don't let young children browse on their own. Second, make sure your children know that they shouldn't give out personal details, such as your address or phone number.

Internet Explorer has its own filtering system, the Content Advisor (find the controls under Tools>Internet Options> Content). However, it only works when Web designers have added ratings to their pages, and most don't. You can't rely on it to protect your children.

Third, you can install filtering programs. These usually do two things: they prevent your children from accessing sites that appear on their blacklist, and they filter out pages containing forbidden words and phrases. Popular filtering programs include:

Cyber Patrol, from SurfControl, at:
`http://www.cyberpatrol.com/`

Net Nanny, from Net Nanny Software International, at:
`http://www.netnanny.com/`

Electronic mail

This chapter introduces Outlook Express, the e-mail program supplied with Windows XP. It shows you how to send and receive messages, add special formatting and attach files. It also explains how to keep track of addresses, sort and file your mail and access Hotmail, Microsoft's Web-based e-mail service.

Covers

Chapter Eight

E-mail explained

E-mail is short for electronic mail, the Internet equivalent of letters and faxes. However, it's better than both of those, not only because it's quick and cheap, but also because you can attach files to an e-mail message. You can send text documents, pictures, sound samples and program files as well as simple messages.

You can send e-mail to anyone on the Internet; you just need to know their address, which will look something like:

johndoe@someplace.co.uk

The part before the @ is the recipient's user name

The part after the @ is the address of the recipient's service provider

When you send an e-mail message, it is delivered to the recipient's service provider very quickly – usually within a couple of minutes. It is stored in the recipient's mail box until he or she next logs on and checks for new e-mail.

E-mail is very efficient if you're dealing with someone who checks their mail box regularly, but not so good for getting messages to people who only log on once a week. It's handy for contacting people who are perpetually on the phone or out of the office and makes it easier to deal with people in different time zones. Instead of calling at an awkward hour, you can have a message waiting for them when they arrive at work.

You can also have news bulletins, reminders and other useful information delivered to your mail box. E-mail might not get as much media coverage as the Web, but it's at least as useful and a lot less time-consuming.

Introducing Outlook Express

Outlook Express is a program for accessing e-mail and Usenet newsgroups (see Chapter 9). It has a few things in common with the Outlook application supplied with Microsoft Office, but don't get the two mixed up. There are differences beneath the surface and things that work in one won't necessarily work in the other. Outlook Express is optimised for sending mail over the Internet, whereas Outlook also has features for communicating with colleagues over a company network.

1 To run Outlook Express, click the Start button and select it from the left-hand side of the Start menu

If you used a CD from your service provider to configure your Internet connection (see page 15), you've probably set up your account already.

2 The first time you do this, you may be prompted to fill in the details of your e-mail account. You'll need to know your e-mail addresses and the addresses of your service provider's mail servers (if you don't have this information, call your service provider)

3 Enter your name

4 Click Next to continue (and after each step)

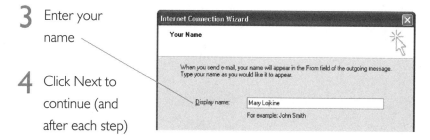

5 Enter your e-mail address

If you want to use Hotmail, Microsoft's Web-based e-mail service, see page 160.

6 Enter the addresses of your service provider's mail servers

When you collect e-mail, you have to send your user name and password twice: once to connect to your service provider and again to access your mail box. Windows XP can automate both log-ins.

7 Fill in your user name and password. Usually these are the same as the ones you use to connect to the Internet (see page 15), but some service providers give you two sets

8 Click Finish. Outlook Express prompts you to connect, then checks for new mail. When it has finished, disconnect (see page 19)

Customising the interface

The Outlook Express window is divided into several panes:

Folder list – folders for all your messages

Toolbar

Contacts list – names from your address book

Main window

1 Select Inbox from the folder list to open your Inbox. The main window is divided in two:

Message list – lists all the messages in this folder

Preview pane – displays the selected message

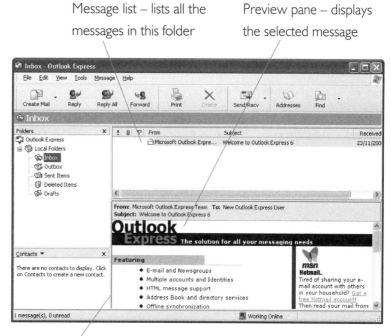

2 Drag the grey dividing bars to adjust the relative sizes of the panes

3 To make further changes, go to View>Layout

4 Select the items you want to display

5 Click Customize Toolbar to add or remove toolbar buttons, change the button size or hide the text labels

Sending e-mail

You have to be connected to the Internet to send a message, but you don't have to be on-line while you compose it. It's best to write your messages before you log on, then send them all in a batch. You can collect any new messages at the same time (see opposite).

Before you write your first message, go to Tools>Options and click the Send tab. Deselect the second option, 'Send messages immediately'. You only want this option selected if you have a permanent connection to the Internet.

1 To write a message, click the Create Mail button, select File>New>Mail Message or press Ctrl+N

2 A New Message window appears

3 Enter the e-mail address of the recipient. You can enter several addresses, separated by semicolons

4 Fill in the 'Subject:' line

If you have one of the Microsoft Office applications, you can spell-check your message. Click the Spelling button, select Tools>Spelling or press F7.

5 Compose your message

6 Click the Send button, select File>Send Message or press Alt+S. This doesn't actually send the message, it just transfers it to the Outbox

7 When you're ready to send your message(s), click the Send/Recv button or press Ctrl+M. Outlook Express connects to the Internet and sends everything in your Outbox

Receiving e-mail

Unlike 'real' mail, e-mail messages aren't automatically delivered to your door – or in this case, computer. When someone sends you an e-mail, it's delivered to your service provider's mail server, which puts it into your personal mail box. You must then log on and collect it.

1 To check your mail box, click Send/Recv. Outlook Express connects to the Internet (if necessary), sends any messages waiting in your Outbox and fetches any new mail. The new messages are placed in your Inbox. You can log off and read them in your own time

See page 156 to find out how to sort your incoming messages.

2 Select the Inbox folder to see the messages you have received

To print a message, click Print, select File>Print or press Ctrl+P.

3 Click once on a message to select it and display the text in the Preview pane at the bottom of the window. Double-click to display it in a separate window

Replying and forwarding

It's easy to reply to an e-mail message, because Internet Explorer automatically adds the correct address.

1 To reply to a message, select it then click the Reply button. Alternatively, select Message>Reply to Sender or press Ctrl+R. Internet Explorer opens a New Message window

Reply

2 The 'To:' and 'Subject:' lines are already filled in

Re: Saturday

File Edit View Insert Format Tools Message Help

Send   Cut   Copy   Paste   Undo   Check   Spelling

To: John Doe
Cc:
Subject: Re: Saturday

Arial   10

Hi John,

If these are the pictures that show me falling off the boat, I'm not s pushed me. Absolutely and without a shadow of a doubt.

I guess that means you owe me a drink.

----- Original Message -----
From: John Doe
To: mary@lojkine.com
Sent: Friday, November 23, 2001 12:04 PM
Subject: Saturday

Hi Mary,

What are you doing on Saturday night? Do you want to meet up pictures back from our diving trip and I could bring them along. Y

John

Quoting is useful when you're dealing with people who receive a lot of mail. If you delete everything except the part of the message to which you're responding, it's easy for them to see what you're on about. However, you can turn this feature off if you find it a nuisance. Go to Tools>Options and click the Send tab. Deselect 'Include message in reply.'

3 The text from the previous message is quoted at the bottom

4 Type your reply

5 Delete any superfluous material from the bottom section, then send the message as usual

Forwarding messages

You can also divert an e-mail message to a friend or to someone who is better able to respond to the sender.

1 To forward a message, select it and click the Forward button. Alternatively, select Message> Forward or press Ctrl+F. Enter the new address in the To: line

Forward

2 Add any comments you wish to make above the quoted text, then send the message

Send and Receive options

Outlook Express' Options dialogue gives you control over when and how messages are sent and received.

Most of the options are fairly easy to understand. For more information, click the Help button ❓ in the top right corner of the dialogue box, then click an option.

1 Select Tools>Options. Click the General tab

2 Select '…at startup' if you want Outlook Express to connect and check for new messages as soon as you run it

3 Select '…every xx minutes' to make Outlook Express check again at regular intervals.
You must also tell it what to do if you aren't on-line at that time

4 Click the Send tab

5 It's courteous to reply to messages in the sender's preferred format

6 Decide whether to create HTML (formatted) or Plain Text messages by default (see overleaf)

7 If you opt for HTML, click the Compose tab to specify a font

Formatted e-mail

Outlook Express enables you to use HTML commands (see page 38) to format your e-mail messages so they look like Web pages.

Formatted mail is fun, and can be useful when you're trying to catch someone's eye. However, it's only a good idea if you're sure the other person uses a program that can handle HTML mail. Formatted messages look awful in older e-mail programs and some people find them irritating. If in doubt, stick to Plain Text (to specify the default format, see Step 6 on the previous page).

1 Use the New Message window's Format menu to switch between Rich Text (HTML) and Plain Text. A formatting bar appears when Rich Text is selected

Stick to fonts that the other person is likely to have: Arial, Comic Sans, Georgia, Impact, Times New Roman, Trebuchet and Verdana.

2 Use the drop-down lists and buttons to format your text

The picture must be saved in the .gif or .jpg format.

3 To add a picture, click Insert Picture [icon] or select Insert>Picture. Click Browse and locate the picture file. Click OK

4 To add a horizontal line, click Insert Horizontal Line ▬ or select Insert>Horizontal Line

You can also insert background sounds, but you'll lose all your friends. No-one wants to receive e-mails that play plinky plonky tunes.

5 To create a fancy backdrop for your text, go to Format> Background. Select Color to choose a solid colour, or Picture to insert an image

Format> Background> Picture inserts an image behind your text. Insert>Picture (Step 3) places the image between paragraphs. Both options have been used in the message on the right. The waves are behind the text, whereas the beach photograph is inserted after the second paragraph.

6 If you're inserting an image, click Browse to locate the file, then click OK

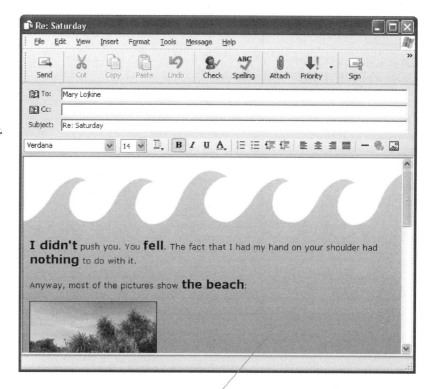

7 The image appears behind your text

Stationery

Outlook Express comes with predesigned Stationery that can add a touch of class to your correspondence or help you celebrate special occasions. As with formatted mail, Stationery is only a good idea if you're sure the recipient's e-mail program can display it.

To specify a default Stationery design, go to Tools>Options. Click the Compose tab, select 'Mail:' and pick a design.

To design your own Stationery, go to Tools> Options and click the Compose tab. Click the Create New button to run the Stationery Wizard.

There's also a Download More button that takes you to Microsoft's Web site, where you'll find lot of extra designs.

1 To compose a new e-mail message using Stationery, click the arrow next to the Create Mail button and select a design

2 The menu only lists a few of the designs. Click Select Stationery for more choices

3 Complete and send your message as usual

Create Mail

1 Clear Day
2 Nature
3 Maize
4 Sunflower
5 Citrus Punch
6 Blank
7 Leaves

Select Stationery...

No Stationery
Web Page...

Autumn leaves

File Edit View Insert Format Tools Message Help

Send | Cut | Copy | Paste | Undo | Check | Spelling | Attach | Priority | Sign | Encrypt

To: John Doe
Cc:
Subject: Autumn leaves

Arial | 14 | B I U A ☰ ☰ ☰ ☰ ☰ ☰ ☰ ☰ — ☰ ☰

Autumn leaves are falling off the trees... can I borrow your broom to sweep them up?

Mary

---

4 If you forget to select a Stationery design when you create your message, make sure Rich Text format is selected (see page 144), then go to Format>Apply Stationery

Signatures

A signature is a short piece of text that is appended to the end of every message you send. If you're sending messages from work, it might include your contact details; otherwise you could use a personal comment or favourite quote. Keep it short, though – long ones soon become tiresome.

You can create several signatures. You might use different ones for business and personal messages. However, you'll have to sign your messages manually – see below.

I Go to Tools> Options and click the Signatures tab

2 Click New

3 Click Rename and give the signature a sensible name

5 Select 'Text' and enter the text you want to add to your messages

If you only want to sign some of your messages, don't select 'Add...'. Instead, use Insert> Signature to add your signature manually before you send your messages.

6 If you want to sign all your messages, select the 'Add signatures to all outgoing messages' option at the top of the dialogue box

7 Click OK

8 The text is added to the end of every message you create

Attachments

You can e-mail pictures, document files and programs to your friends and colleagues. If you have a digital camera or microphone, you can bring your messages to life with snapshots or recordings. More prosaically, being able to exchange files by e-mail is handy if you're working from home.

1 Compose your message (see page 140) and click the Attach button. Alternatively, select File Attachment from the New Message window's Insert menu

You can attach any kind of file, but don't send your friends large files without warning them first. You should also make sure they have the right software for viewing your files.

2 Find the file(s) you want to send – you can select several files at once by holding down Shift or Ctrl

3 Click Attach

If you change your mind about one of the files, right-click on its entry in the 'Attach:' line, then select Remove from the pop-up menu.

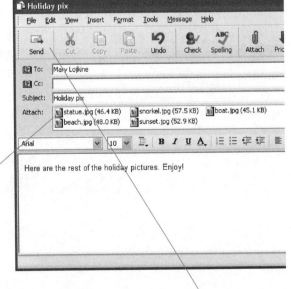

4 The files are added to the message

5 Send the message in the usual way

...cont'd

Receiving attachments

When you receive a message with attached files, you have two main choices: open the files, or save them onto your hard disk.

If you receive a file from someone you don't know, don't open it. The safest option is to delete the entire message. Alternatively, save the file on to your hard disk and check for viruses before you open it. This also applies to Word and Excel documents, which can carry macro viruses (see page 121).

1 If you see paperclip icons in the message list and preview pane, the associated message has one or more files attached. In some cases – for example, when a .gif or .jpg image has been attached – the file is displayed at the end of the text

2 When you open the message, the attached files are listed at the top. Right-click a file to open or save it

3 You can also deal with attached files by clicking the yellow paperclip at the top of the Preview Pane. Click a file to open it, or click Save Attachments to save the files on to your hard disk

4 Click Browse and choose a folder

5 Select the files you want to save and click Save

Address Book

The Address Book enables you to store all the e-mail addresses you use regularly. You can then add them to messages more easily.

1 To open the Address Book, click the Addresses button, select Tools>Address Book or press Ctrl+Shift+B

Addresses

It's even easier to add the address of someone who has sent you an e-mail message. Select the message, then go to Tools>Add Sender to Address Book.

2 To add an address, click the New button and select New Contact. You can also select File>New Contact or press Ctrl+N

3 Fill in the person's name and (optionally) nickname

4 Enter their e-mail address and click Add. Repeat if they have several

6 Click the Home, Business, Personal and Other tabs to add any extra information you wish to record

7 Click OK to finish

To access the Address Book from the New Message window, click the icon 📖 *to the left of the 'To:' or 'Cc:' lines.*

8 You can now enter the person's name or nickname in the 'To:' line of your messages. Outlook Express will look up the address when you send the message. Alternatively, double-click the person's entry in the Contacts list to create a pre-addressed message form

Mailing groups

Mailing groups make it easy to send messages to several people.

Suppose you belong to a football team, and it's your job to e-mail the others with details of the next match. Instead of going through your address book, selecting each name, you can set up a mailing group that contains all the e-mail addresses. When you want to send a message to everyone, you address it to the group.

1 Open the Address Book. Click the New button and select New Group

When you send a message to a mailing group, you send it to everyone in that group. If you select a mailing group by accident, you can embarrass yourself by broadcasting a private message to everyone you know. Be careful!

2 Give the mailing group a name

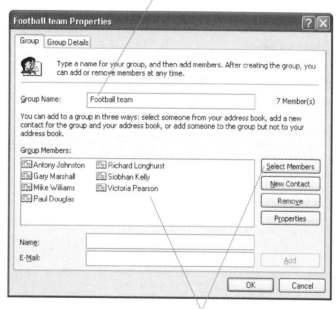

Football team Properties

Group | Group Details

Type a name for your group, and then add members. After creating the group, you can add or remove members at any time.

Group Name: Football team   7 Member(s)

You can add to a group in three ways: select someone from your address book, add a new contact for the group and your address book, or add someone to the group but not to your address book.

Group Members:

Antony Johnston   Richard Longhurst
Gary Marshall   Siobhan Kelly
Mike Williams   Victoria Pearson
Paul Douglas

[Select Members]
[New Contact]
[Remove]
[Properties]

Name:
E-Mail: [Add]

[OK] [Cancel]

Use the 'Name' and 'E-mail' boxes at the bottom of the New Group dialogue box to add people to the group without adding them to your Address Book.

3 To add people from your Address Book, click Select Members

4 Click OK to finish

5 To send a message to everyone in the group, double-click its entry in your Contacts list

Contacts ▼
David Crouch
Football team
Gary Marshall
Harshad Kotecha
Ian Sanders
Ian White

vCards

A vCard is an electronic business card. It enables you to send personal information to other Internet users, in a format that their Address Book can understand.

1 To create a vCard, you must first create an Address Book entry (see page 150) with your own information. Include your home and/or business details if you wish to share them

This convoluted procedure tells Outlook Express which Address Book entry you would choose if you wanted to add a vCard to every outgoing message. That would be overkill, so you should deselect the 'Mail:' checkbox (Step 3). Outlook Express remembers which entry you chose, but only adds the vCard when you instruct it to do so (Step 4).

2 Go back to Outlook Express and select Tools>Options. Click the Compose tab. In the Business Cards section, select the 'Mail:' checkbox. Select your name from the drop-down list

3 Deselect the 'Mail:' checkbox and click OK

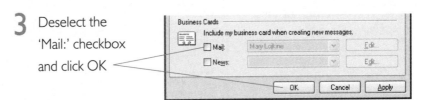

4 To attach your vCard to an outgoing message, select Insert>My Business Card

If you open the message in its own window, a smaller version of the icon appears at the right-hand end of the 'From:' line.

5 When you receive a message with a vCard, click the icon that appears in the top right-hand corner of the Preview pane. Choose the 'Open it' option and click OK

6 The information in the vCard is displayed. Click the Add to Address Book button to transfer it to your Address Book

Managing your e-mail

Initially you have five e-mail folders: Inbox, Outbox, Sent Items, Deleted Items and Drafts.

1   New e-mail is deposited in the Inbox (see page 141)

2   Outgoing e-mail waits in the Outbox (see page 140)

3   Once a message has been dispatched, it is moved to the Sent Items folder so you have a copy

The Deleted Items folder is like the Windows Recycle Bin – it stores items you think you won't need again until you're ready to get rid of them for good. To empty the folder, select Edit>Empty 'Deleted Items' Folder.

4   If you select a message and click Delete, select Edit> Delete, press Delete or press Ctrl+D, it ends up in the Deleted Items folder. You can rescue it if necessary

5   If you close a message without sending it, Outlook Express asks if you want to save the changes. Click Yes to move the message to the Drafts folder so you can finish writing it later on.

Sorting your e-mail

As well as placing your e-mail in these folders, Outlook Express enables you to sort the messages in each one.

To change the column headings, right-click on one of the tabs and select Columns...

To sort your messages, click one of the grey tabs at the top of the list. Click again to reverse the sort

A small grey arrow within the tab tells you which column is being used to sort the messages. It points upwards for a regular sort and downwards for a reverse sort.

Sorted by sender   Sorted by date received

Creating your own folders

Some messages can be thrown away as soon as you've read them, but there'll be others you want to keep. You can create additional e-mail folders and file them away tidily.

1 To create a new e-mail folder, go to File>Folder>New

2 Enter a name

If the folder ends up in the wrong place, use the mouse to drag it around the Folder list.

3 To create a new top-level folder, select Local Folders. To add a subfolder, select one of your existing folders

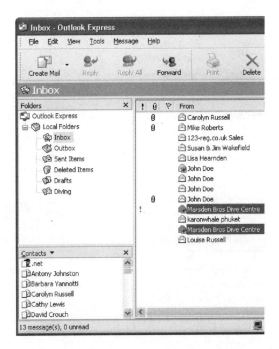

4 Click OK to add the folder to the Folder list

5 Use the mouse to drag messages into the new folder. You can also select them (hold down Shift or Ctrl to select several at once), then go to Edit> Move to Folder. Select the folder and click OK

Finding messages

No matter how careful you are when you file your e-mail, there will come a day when you can't find the message where so-and-so said such-and-such. Outlook Express' Find function can usually track down the missing message – assuming it hasn't been permanently deleted.

1 To search for a message, go to Edit>Find>Message. Alternatively, press Ctrl+Shift+F

If you're reasonably certain that the message is in a particular folder, select it (rather than Local Folders) when you click the Browse button. The search will be restricted to that folder and Outlook Express should find the message more quickly.

2 Click the Browse button and select Local Folders to search everywhere. Make sure 'Include subfolders' is selected

3 Enter all the details you're sure about. Use the 'Message:' line for words that appeared in the text of the message

4 Click the Find Now button

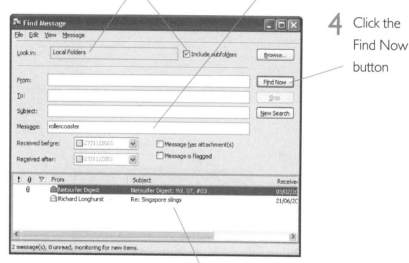

5 Outlook Express searches for matching messages and lists them at the bottom of the box. Double-click a message to open it

6 If you get a long list of messages, enter more details and click Find Now again. Conversely, if you don't get any matches, try entering less information. A single, well-chosen word may be enough

Message Rules

Message Rules enable you to sort your incoming messages by sender, subject or content and automatically highlight, file, delete or reply to them. They're useful for separating business and personal mail, or for blocking messages from people who keep sending you junk.

1 To create a Message Rule, go to Tools>Message Rules>Mail. Click the New button

You can select several conditions and actions at once to create very complex Rules. The dialogue boxes that enable you to specify the details of each condition usually have Options buttons that give you even more choices. For example, you can reverse the Rule so the action is applied when the message doesn't meet your condition.

2 Select a condition that the message must meet

3 Select the action to be taken

4 Click the blue, underlined text to fill in details of the condition

5 Fill in details of the action

6 Give the Rule a name and click OK

There are two easy ways to create Rules based on the sender of the message. Select a message from the correct person, then go to Message> Create Rule From Message to bring up the New Mail Rule box with the 'From' details already specified. Alternatively, you can ignore this person by selecting Message>Block Sender.

7 All your Rules are listed in the Message Rules dialogue box

8 Use the checkboxes to enable or disable any of your Rules

9 Rules are applied in order. Click Move Up or Move Down to reshuffle them

10 Click a Rule to see its details

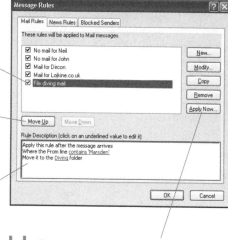

11 Click Apply Now to test your Rules

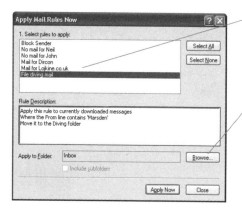

12 Select the Rule(s) you want to test

13 Click Browse to pick a folder – your Inbox is usually the best choice

14 Click Apply Now to proceed with the test

15 Close all the dialogue boxes and check whether your Rule has had the desired effect. If not, go back to the Message Rules dialogue box and select the Rule. Click Modify to change the condition and/ or action

16 The active Rules (see Step 8) are applied to all your incoming mail

Multiple accounts

Outlook Express also has a feature called Identities which enables two or more people to use the program without mixing up their e-mail. This feature has been superseded by the User Accounts system built in to Windows XP.

It's quite common to have more than one e-mail account. Many service providers give you several e-mail addresses, and the rise of free services has encouraged people to sign up for several Internet accounts. There's no point getting carried away, but it is useful to have separate addresses for business and personal mail.

1. To add a new account, select Tools>Accounts. Click Add and select Mail

2. The Internet Connection Wizard asks you questions about your account (see pages 137–138)

3. You'll end up back at the Internet Accounts dialogue box, with your new account added to the list

Messages are dispatched from your default e-mail account unless you specify otherwise.

4. Select your main account and click Set as Default

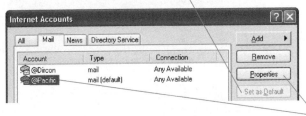

5. To change the details you entered in Step 2, select the account and click Properties

The 'Include this account when...' option determines whether this account is checked when you click Send/Receive. If you only want to check for mail occasionally, deselect this checkbox.

6. The General section has your personal details. The name you enter here is the one people will see when you send them a message

...cont'd

If you have e-mail accounts with several Internet service providers, you may need to specify the correct connection for each one. Some service providers only let you send mail when you are connected directly.

7 The Connection section tells Outlook Express how to log on to the Internet when you click Send/Receive

Using your accounts

You can send and receive mail from your default account in the usual way. Using secondary accounts is slightly more complicated.

1 If the 'Include this account when...' option is selected (see the 'HOT TIP' on the opposite page), the new account is checked

when you click Send and Receive. If not, you must check it manually. Go to Tools>Send and Receive, then select the account

The 'From:' list only appears when you have more than one account.

2 To send a message from a particular account, select it from the drop-down 'From:' list at the top of the New Message form

Hotmail

Hotmail is a free e-mail system owned by Microsoft. It's designed to be used from a Web browser, so you can access your e-mail from any computer that's connected to the Internet, without having to set up an e-mail program. It's useful if you are travelling or want to send personal messages from a company computer.

The downside of Web-based mail systems such as Hotmail is that you have to be on-line to read or write messages. However, recent versions of Outlook Express provide a solution: you can download the messages on to your computer and respond to them off-line. This setup gives you the best of both worlds. When you're away from home, you can read your mail via the Web. When you get back, you can use Outlook Express instead.

To create a new Hotmail account, go to Hotmail's Web site at http://www.hotmail.com/ Click the links in the 'All About Hotmail' section to find out more about the service, then choose a user name and password. If you don't already have a .NET Passport (see page 130), you'll end up creating one along the way.

Once that's done, configure Outlook Express to access your Hotmail account.

1 Follow Steps 1 and 2 on page 158 to start the Internet Connection Wizard. Enter your name and Hotmail address

2 When you're asked what type of server you use, select HTTP. Select Hotmail from the drop-down list.

3 Outlook Express fills in the server details for you

4 When you get back to
the Accounts dialogue
box, click the Close
button. You'll be asked if
you want to download folders from the server. Click Yes

5 A new set of folders appears at the bottom of the Folders list

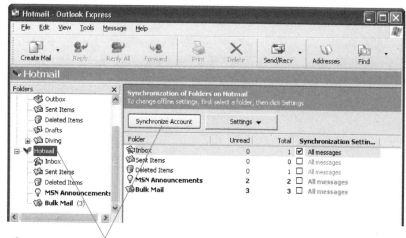

6 To check for new messages, select the Hotmail folder, then click
Synchronize Account. Outlook Express checks the Web server and
downloads any new messages to your computer

7 To send a message, click Create Mail, then select your Hotmail
account from the 'From:' list

Making the most of e-mail

E-mail isn't just a way to bypass the postbox and fax machine. It also enables you to keep informed, join discussion groups, play games and have some fun with your friends.

The easiest way to fill your Inbox is by subscribing to mailing lists. There are two sorts: announcement lists that deliver regular newsletter-style messages, and discussion lists that are more like e-mail conversations. Everyone on the list submits their news, thoughts, recipes or whatever to the mail server, which copies them to all the members. They're a good way to get in touch with Internet users who share your interests.

Many of the bigger Web sites have announcement lists that tell you what has been added each week. You can usually sign up somewhere on the site – in fact, you'll often find that registering (see page 51) puts you on the list. Discussion lists may also have associated Web pages, but you usually sign up by e-mail. Get started by visiting the Topica Web site, which catalogues thousands of mailing lists. Find it at:
`http://www.topica.com/`

Play-by-e-mail games are also popular. You can get involved in everything from board, strategy and role-playing games to fantasy sports leagues. Some games work entirely by e-mail – you submit your move and wait for a response – while others take moves by e-mail, then display the results on a Web site.

Finally, there are lots of Web sites that use e-mail to deliver useful or amusing services. You can send electronic postcards to your friends, use automatic letter writers to generate romantic or sarcastic messages, or order a (picture of) a pizza over the Web. On a more practical note, you can sign up for reminder services that send you messages on (or just before) important dates such as birthdays and anniversaries. Go to Yahoo! (see page 78) and search for 'e-mail' or 'cards' to find out what's available.

Usenet newsgroups

Usenet newsgroups enable you to communicate with Internet users who share your interests. This chapter shows you how to read and post messages. It also explains newsgroup etiquette and customs.

Covers

Chapter Nine

Newsgroups explained

The Usenet newsgroups are the Internet equivalent of your local pub or social club. They aren't as pretty as the Web, but they're interactive. If you're looking for gossip, trivia, advice, arguments and – very occasionally – news, Usenet is the place to find it.

Newsgroup messages are also referred to as 'posts' and 'articles'. The three terms are interchangeable.

You can think of a newsgroup as a public mail box for messages on a particular topic. Anyone can post a comment, and anyone else can read it and upload a reply.

Unlike Web pages, newsgroups aren't stored in any particular place. All the messages are copied from one news server to the next, enabling you to access them locally. Rather than connecting to lots of sites from all over the globe, you download the latest messages from your Service Provider's news server.

There are over 50,000 newsgroups, although some service providers only carry the more popular ones. Some have a close-knit community of regular posters; others are larger and more anonymous. Either way, there's certain to be someone who wants to share your experiences, answer your questions, ask for advice or just pass the time of day.

Understanding newsgroup names

Newsgroup addresses look like:
`rec.arts.movies.reviews`

or sometimes:
`news:rec.arts.movies.reviews`

Newsgroups are organised hierarchically: each section of the address (moving from left to right) reduces the scope of the group. In this case `rec` stands for recreation, `arts` and `movies` are self-evident and the group only carries `reviews`. There are a dozen other `movies` groups, about 130 other `arts` groups, and over 800 `rec` groups in total.

`rec` is only one of dozens of top-level categories. However, you can find almost everything you're likely to want in `alt`, `comp`, `news`, `rec`, `sci`, `soc` and `uk`.

alt – alternative

Almost anyone can create an `alt` newsgroup, so the `alt` hierarchy is one of the liveliest sections of Usenet. Some of the groups are pretty wild, but most are just odd – if you're interested in alien conspiracies, urban legends or breakfast cereal, `alt` has plenty to offer. It's also a nursery for new groups, some of which eventually graduate to the more respectable hierarchies.

comp – computing

The `comp` groups deal with everything from hardware and software to artificial intelligence and home automation.

news – Usenet

The `news` groups are for discussion about Usenet. They aren't terribly exciting, but `news.announce.newusers` has lots of information for beginners.

The name 'Usenet' is derived from 'User Network.'

Usenet is a network of computers (news servers) that exchange news messages.

rec – recreation

The `rec` groups cover hobbies, sports, arts and music, and are the best place to start. They are friendlier than the `alt` groups and it's easy to find your way around.

sci – science

The `sci` groups cover mathematics, physics, engineering, chemistry, biological science, medicine, psychology and philosophy – everything except computing, basically.

soc – social

The `soc` groups deal with social issues. The biggest subsection, `soc.culture`, has over 100 groups dedicated to different countries and cultures. Genealogy, history and religion are well represented and there are several support groups.

uk – United Kingdom

The uk groups are a microcosm of Usenet as a whole. The busiest groups are `uk.people.gothic` and `uk.jobs.offered`, but you'll also find an *Archers* group, assorted political groups and a selection of `rec` and `religion` groups.

Getting started

There are many similarities between sending e-mail and posting messages to newsgroups. You use Outlook Express for both, and many operations are identical. However, you will notice some changes in the menus when you switch from sending and receiving e-mail to reading news.

The first thing you need to do is find out the address of your service provider's news server and set up Outlook Express to connect to it.

1   Run Outlook Express and select Tools>Accounts. Click Add and select News

2   Enter your name and e-mail address, clicking Next after each step

3   Fill in the address of your service provider's news server. You don't normally have to log on to news servers

4   When you get back to the Internet Accounts dialogue box, click the News tab. You should see an entry for your news server. Select it and click the Properties button to give it a sensible name

5   When you close the dialogue box, Outlook Express asks if you want to download newsgroups. Click Yes

6 Outlook Express downloads the names of the newsgroups carried by your service provider. This takes a few minutes, but you only have to do it once

Subscribing to a newsgroup isn't like subscribing to a magazine or joining a club. You don't have to pay, and you won't be added to a membership list. Subscribing just tells Outlook Express you're interested in a newsgroup – it's like making a Favorite for a Web site.

7 The newsgroup list appears. You need to select some newsgroups and 'subscribe' to them

8 Scroll down the list until you find a group that looks interesting, then select it and click the Subscribe button

9 To find groups covering a particular subject, type a word that might appear in the name into the 'Display...' box

10 Click the Subscribed tab to see a list of the groups you have selected

11 If you want to add more groups later on, select your news server from the Folders list. Click the Newsgroups button or select Tools>Newsgroups. You won't have to download the list again

Reading news

Reading newsgroup messages is slightly different from reading e-mail. Instead of downloading all the messages, which might take some time, Outlook Express only fetches the headers (the subject line, name of sender and so on). You then download the ones that sound interesting.

1 Select your news server from the Folder list to display your subscribed newsgroups

Some groups are very busy and receive hundreds of new messages each day. To tell Outlook Express how many headers to fetch, select Tools> Options and click the Read tab. Enter a number in the 'Get xx headers...' box.

2 Double-click one of the groups to download the titles of the messages

3 Click a title to download and display the body of the message

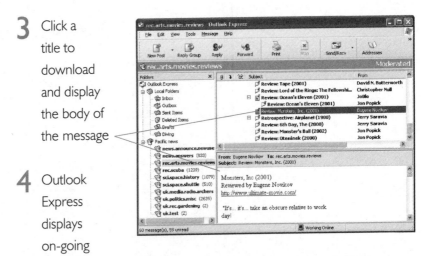

4 Outlook Express displays on-going conversations as 'threads', with the responses immediately below the original message. Click the plus ⊞ and minus ⊟ icons to expand and contract the threads

Posting messages

See page 174 before you start posting messages – there are lots of things that are considered rude on Usenet.

Posting messages is similar to sending e-mail (see page 140), but you address the message to the newsgroup.

I To create a new message, ensure you are viewing the right newsgroup. Click New Post, select Message>New Message or press Ctrl+N

HOT TIP
If your response won't be of interest to anyone other than the original poster, e-mail it directly to them. Click Reply to Author, select Message>Reply to Sender or press Ctrl+R to create a pre-addressed form.

2 To respond to a message, select it. Click Reply to Group, select Message>Reply to Group or press Ctrl+G

3 Either way, Outlook Express launches a pre-addressed New Message window (if it's a response to an existing message, the original text is quoted – see page 142). Fill in the Subject line and compose your message

HOT TIP
Want to practise? Post a message to the alt.test or uk.test newsgroups. These groups were created for people who want to experiment with their software.

4 Click Send, select File>Send Later or press Alt+S to transfer the message to your Outbox

5 Your message is uploaded to the news server when you click Send/Receive or Synchronize Account

Working off-line

To minimise the amount of time spent on-line, mark the messages you want to read and download them all at once. You can then disconnect from the Internet and read messages off-line.

1 | Select your news server from the Folder list

News messages don't stay on the server forever; your service provider keeps clearing them out to make way for new ones. If a group is very busy, they may only be accessible for a day or two, so check popular groups regularly. You can also use Google Groups (see page 80) to read old posts.

2 | Select all your newsgroups, then click the Settings button and select Headers Only

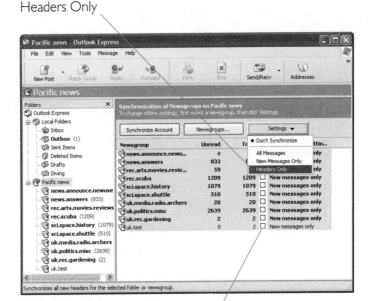

3 | Deselect the checkboxes of any groups you don't want to bother with today

4 | Click Synchronize Account. Outlook Express connects to the Internet and downloads the headers of any new messages sent to any of the selected groups

5 | Log off and select Work Offline from the File menu

6 | Double-click on one of your newsgroups. Scroll down the list of messages and select one that sounds interesting

...cont'd

If you read more than half the messages posted to a group, you're better off selecting New Messages Only (rather than Headers) in Step 2 and fetching everything. Use the Headers option at least once before you do this, though. If you don't, all the messages will be new and you might have to download thousands of them.

7 Mark the message for downloading. To do this, go to Tools>Mark for Offline>Download Message Later. You can also mark an entire conversation (thread), or all the messages in the group

You can mark messages more quickly by clicking in the column where the arrows appear.

8 Mark all the other interesting messages, then repeat for the other newsgroups. Marked messages have blue arrows ↓

9 When you've finished, select Tools>Synchronize All or go back to the list of groups and click the Synchronize Account button again

10 Outlook Express downloads the marked messages

11 Log off and select Work Offline again. Select a newsgroup, then select one of the messages you marked. You'll be able to display the message in the Preview Pane

Views

Outlook Express keeps newsgroup messages on your hard disk for the number of days specified under Tools> Options>Maintenance.

After a few days, you'll have downloaded lots of messages. Outlook Express displays the headers of the ones you haven't read in a bold font. Read messages are listed in a plain font so you can see the difference. Finding the new ones can still be a chore, though.

1 To make things easier, switch Views so only the messages you haven't read are displayed. To do this, go to View>Current View>Hide Read Messages

To see only the messages that can be read off-line, select View> Current View>Show Downloaded Messages.

2 To get the older messages back so you can see the new ones in context, select Show All Messages

Turn on the Views bar (from View>Layout) for quick access to all the different Views.

3 You can also make boring conversations go away. Select the earliest message in the thread, then go to Message>Ignore Conversation

4 When you set the Current View to Hide Read or Ignored Messages, the entire conversation disappears

Message Rules

Message Rules for newsgroups are much like Message Rules for e-mail (see page 156), except they're used to highlight or ignore messages, rather than to file them.

1 Go to Tools>Message Rules>News and click the New button

2 Choose the conditions. Usually you'll want to specify a newsgroup *and* select another condition, such as the subject

3 Select the action

4 Click the blue, underlined text to fill in the details

5 Name the Rule

If you get fed up with an individual and want to ignore all of their messages, select one, then go to Message>Block Sender. Users of other programs call this 'kill-filing.'

6 The Rule is applied to all the messages you receive from now on. This one has removed the 'retrospective' reviews of older films.

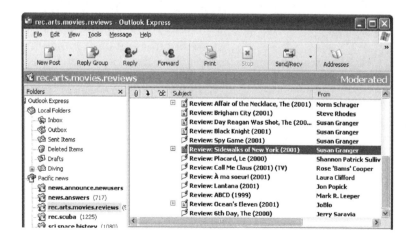

Netiquette

Usenet has a reputation for being hostile to beginners or 'newbies'. While it's true that some groups are hard to break into, most welcome anyone who displays a little common sense and courtesy. In particular, try to adhere to the following guidelines, known collectively as 'Netiquette'.

A 'flame' is an abusive message. Some groups tolerate and even encourage flaming; others expect members to be civil. If you post a flame, be prepared to get flamed back!

1   Always read the FAQ (see the facing page) before you start posting messages, to avoid (a) posting messages that are inappropriate and (b) asking questions that have already been answered hundreds of times.

2   Avoid posting the same message to several groups at once. This is known as 'cross posting', and it irritates the people who end up downloading your message several times.

3   Don't ever post the same message to lots and lots of newsgroups. This is known as 'spamming', and it irritates everyone. Sadly, you'll encounter lots of spam on Usenet, especially in the `alt` groups. Ignore it – responding just makes things worse.

4   Don't post Rich Text messages (see page 144), because most newsreading software won't display them properly. Stick to Plain Text.

For more advice on how to stay in line on-line, see 'Using the Internet in easy steps pocket', also published by Computer Step.

5   If you're replying to a message, don't quote more of the original than is necessary – most people won't want to read it all again. It's helpful to quote the sentence or two you're actually responding to, though.

6   Avoid posting messages that just say, 'Me too,' or, 'I agree.' Wait until you have something interesting to contribute.

7   Don't type your message in upper case. This is known as SHOUTING, AND IT MAKES YOUR MESSAGE DIFFICULT TO READ.

8   If you use a signature (see page 147), keep it short. Four lines is considered the maximum acceptable length.

FAQs

A FAQ is a compilation of Frequently Asked Questions – and their answers. FAQs exist for two reasons: to set out the group's scope and rules, and to answer all the questions a newcomer might ask.

'Lurkers' read the messages in a newsgroup, but don't post anything. It's a good way to find out what is acceptable in a particular newsgroup.

Most FAQs are posted regularly, generally weekly or monthly. If you 'lurk' in a newsgroup for a while, the FAQ should eventually appear. You can also find FAQs for many newsgroups in the Internet FAQ Archives at:

`http://www.faqs.org/faqs/`

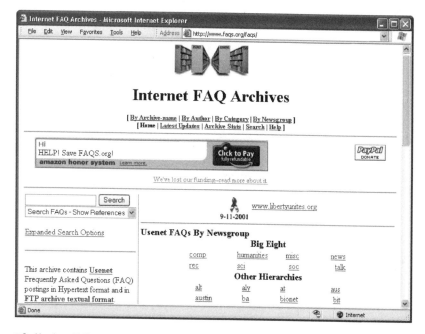

If all else fails, post a polite message asking someone to point you in the right direction. Some groups don't have FAQs; others have more than one, and some FAQs serve several groups. If you can't find a FAQ, lurk for a week or two to get a feel for the group.

Many FAQs represent the collective knowledge of the members of the newsgroup, and they can be fascinating reading in their own right. The question-and-answer format has also become popular elsewhere on the Internet – Web sites often have FAQ pages.

Smileys and acronyms

Smileys and acronyms speed things up and help you clarify your comments.

Smileys

Smileys are also known as 'emoticons'. Don't use too many – some people think they're silly.

It's difficult to communicate your emotions in a brief text message to a stranger. This can lead to misunderstandings, particularly if you are prone to bluntness or sarcasm. Consequently, some people use 'smileys' – little faces made out of keyboard characters – to convey their state of mind.

There are many, many smileys. The three you're most likely to encounter are:

:-)	happy
;-)	winking or 'only joking'
:-(	sad or disappointed

(Turn the book through 90 degrees clockwise to see the faces.)

Acronyms

Common phrases are often abbreviated to their initials, producing TLAs (Three-Letter Acronyms) and ETLAs (Extended TLAs). You'll also see phonetic abbreviations.

Found an acronym that you can't decipher? Try the Acronym Finder, at: http://www.acronymfinder.com/

Common acronyms and abbreviations include:

AFAIK	As far as I know
B4	Before
BTW	By the way
F2F	Face to face
FYI	For your information
<g>	Grin
IMO	In my opinion
IMHO	In my humble opinion
IMNSHO	In my not so humble opinion
ISTM	It seems to me
ISTR	I seem to recall
IRL	In real life (meaning, off the Internet)
L8R	Later
ROFL	Rolling on floor laughing
RSN	Real soon now
RTFM	Read the 'flipping' manual

Windows Messenger

Windows Messenger enables you to chat with other Internet users, either by typing comments or by speaking into a microphone. This chapter shows you how to contact your friends and exchange messages and files. It also explains how to conduct voice conversations over the Internet.

Covers

Chapter Ten

Introducing instant messaging

As the name suggests, instant-messaging programs enable you to send messages to other Internet users, instantly. Whereas an e-mail message may languish in their mail box for hours or even days, an instant message pops on to their screen straight away – assuming they are connected to the Internet and have activated their messaging program. The big difference between instant messaging and e-mail is that messaging enables people *who are on-line* to communicate with other people *who are on-line*. It's a real-time, interactive service that needs a live connection.

When you run an instant-messaging program, it notifies a central server that you're on-line and ready to receive messages. The server acts as a giant, global 'in/out' board and keeps track of everyone's status. However, you don't have to hunt through millions of names to find out whether your friends are on-line. Your messaging program automatically checks the status of your 'contacts' or 'buddies' and displays a list of people you can send messages to. This system makes instant messaging one of the simplest and friendliest Internet applications. The software tells you who is available, and you double-click their name to send a message. There are no addresses to remember (or forget).

Introducing Windows Messenger

MSN Messenger is also available for Pocket PCs and Apple Macintoshes.

The instant-messaging program included with Windows XP is called Windows Messenger. If your friends use Windows 95, 98, Me, NT 4.0 or 2000, they can install a similar program called MSN Messenger. It doesn't have Windows Messenger's more advanced features, but it enables people who use older versions of Windows to exchange messages with people who use Windows XP.

This chapter explains how to use Windows Messenger. To obtain the latest release for use with Windows XP, you'll need to download it from the Windows Update Web site (see page 106), or from the .NET Messenger Service Web site, at:
`http://messenger.microsoft.com/`

If your friends need to download MSN Messenger, they can get it from the same address.

You'll also need a .NET Passport (see page 130).

Getting started

When you start Windows, it may run Windows Messenger automatically. If it doesn't, you can start the program manually.

1 Look for an icon showing a green, stylised person in the notification area at the right-hand end of the taskbar. Double-click it to open the program window

2 If you can't find the icon, click the Start button and select All Programs, then Windows Messenger

3 Either way, Windows Messenger may prompt you to sign in

4 If you don't have a .NET Passport, you'll be asked to create one (see page 130)

If you select the 'Sign me in automatically' option, you won't have to enter your details next time.

5 If you do have a Passport, enter your e-mail address and password

6 Click OK to sign in

7 Windows Messenger contacts the central server and informs it that you're on-line and ready to receive messages

If you have a standard installation of Windows XP and have created a Passport, Windows Messenger may sign you in automatically. You'll go straight to the screen shown in Step 1 overleaf.

Adding contacts

The next thing to do is add your friends to your Contacts list, so you can send messages to them easily. You'll need to know their e-mail addresses.

You should see your name at the top of the window. If you'd rather use a nickname, go to Tools>Options and click the Personal tab. Change the 'My display name' setting.

If your friend has more than one e-mail address, you'll need to find out which one they use for their .NET Passport.

1 Click the 'Add a Contact' link in the 'I want to...' list at the bottom of the window

2 Select 'By e-mail address or sign-in name'

3 Click Next (and click it again after each step)

4 Enter your friend's e-mail address

5 Windows Messenger checks with the central server and tries to locate your friend. If it is successful, their name is added to your Contact list

6 If your friend isn't using Windows Messenger, you can't add them to your list. You're invited to send them an e-mail that explains how to download and install it

When you add someone to your Contacts list (Step 4), Windows Messenger lets them know. They have two options: they can allow you to contact them, or block all your messages. Likewise, when someone adds you to their list, you can let them in or shut them out. This prevents total strangers from bothering you with irrelevant messages.

1 If you know the person and want to communicate with them, select 'Allow this person…' You can add them to your own Contact list

2 If you've been added by someone you don't know (or don't like), choose 'Block this person…'

3 If you change your mind about someone, go to Tools>Options. Click the Privacy tab and move the person from the Allow list to the Block list, or vice versa

Exchanging messages

Windows Messenger divides your contacts into two groups: people who are on-line, and people who aren't. Simply glance at the list to find out who is available.

1 To contact one of your friends, double-click on their name

2 Type a message into the bottom window

3 Click Send

4 The message pops up on the other person's screen. If they feel like chatting, you'll get a reply in a few seconds

5 The reply appears in the top window

If you can't type well, use abbreviations to speed things up. Try 'u' for 'you', 'cu' for 'see you' and '18r' for 'later'.

6 To carry on chatting, type another comment into the bottom window and click Send again

...cont'd

All the icons have keyboard shortcuts. To see the complete list, click the Emoticons button, then click the button with three dots ☐ See page 176 for more about emoticons.

7 To convey humour or emotion, click the Emoticons button and choose an icon

When one of your friends tries to contact you, the initial message pops up in the bottom right-hand corner of your screen.

1 Click the message to bring up the Conversation window

Once you've started a conversation, you can invite up to three more people to join in. Go to the 'I want to...' list on the right-hand side of the Conversation window and click the 'Invite Someone to this Conversation' link. Select the person you want to add, then click OK.

2 Carry on with the conversation by typing a reply into the bottom window

Sending files

As well as exchanging messages, you can share files or photographs.

1   To send a file, start a conversation and then click the 'Send a file or photo link'

Remember that large files take a long time to transfer. As a rough guide, a 250K file takes about a minute if you're using a 56kbps modem and have a good connection.

2   Find the file and click Open

3   Wait for the other person to accept the file. When they do, the transfer begins

When someone tries to send you a file, Windows Messenger tells you how big it is and how long it will take to transfer.

1   To accept the file, click Accept. To refuse it, click Decline

You should only open the file if you trust the person who sent it. If you have any doubts, use a virus checker to scan the file for viruses before you open it.

2   If you accept the file, it is transferred to your hard disk. Click the link to open it

Voice conversations

If you aren't much of a typist, typed conversations can be frustratingly slow. One alternative is to set up a microphone and hold voice conversations instead. It's much like using the telephone, except that the sounds travel from computer to computer, over the Internet. The sound quality isn't quite what you'd expect during a regular telephone call, but because the conversation is carried over the Internet, you can speak to computer users anywhere in the world for the price of the call that connects you to your service provider.

To improve the sound quality, invest in a headset microphone – a set of headphones with an attached microphone.

1 Before you can hold voice conversations, you need to set up your speakers and microphone. Make sure they are plugged in and switched on, then run Windows Messenger. Go to Tools>Audio Tuning Wizard and follow the on-screen instructions to fine-tune the volume settings

You can also speak to people who don't have computers. However, you'll need to open an account with a voice service provider – a company that connects Internet-originated calls to regular telephones. Select the 'Make a Phone Call' option for more details.

2 To speak to one of your friends, click 'Start a Voice Conversation'

3 Select the person you want to call, then click OK. Your friend receives an instant message inviting them to talk to you

4 Once your friend has accepted the invitation, start speaking

5 Use the sliders to adjust the speaker and microphone volumes

6 You can type into the bottom window as you speak. This is handy if you're sharing names or phone numbers

Other ways to communicate

You can also send and receive video (assuming you have a video camera), draw pictures on a communal whiteboard and share applications and games. You can even let a more knowledgeable friend take control of your computer, from a distance, to sort out a problem for you.

These options work best over high-speed, broadband connections (see page 11). They're only available when both parties are running Windows XP. If your friend has an older version of Windows and is using MSN Messenger (see page 178), you can't use any of these features. You'll have to stick to typed or spoken conversations, at least until they upgrade.

For information about the more advanced features of Windows Messenger, bring up the main window and select Help>Help Topics. Click the 'All Topics' link at the top of the page to display the table of contents.

Index

D

Default
  Connection 20
  E-mail account 158
Deleted Items folder 153
Delia Online (site) 98
Dell (site) 102
Diamond (site) 102
Director. *See* Shockwave
Directories 78
Disconnecting
  Automatically 21
  From the Internet 19, 21
Discovery Channel Online (site) 100
Domain names 27
Dotmusic (site) 88
Downloading
  Extra components 122
  MSN Messenger 178
  Newsgroup list 166
  Newsgroup messages 168, 170
  Pages for browsing off-line 63
  Program files 45–46
  Sound 42
  Video 42
  Web pages 29
  Windows Media Player 44
  Windows Messenger 178
Drafts folder 153

E

E-mail
  Accounts 158
  Addresses 136, 150
  Attachments 148–149
  Composing 140
  Folders 154
  Formatting 144
  Forwarding 142
  Introduction to 9, 136
  Making the most of 162
  Managing 153
  Printing 141
  Receiving 141, 143, 159
  Replying to 142
  Searching 155
  Sending 140, 143, 159
  Sorting 153, 156
  Spell-checking 140
E-zines 90

Easy as 1-2-Free (site) 82
Economist, The (site) 89
Electronic mail. *See* E-mail
Emoticons 176, 183
Empire Online (site) 86
Encyclopædia Britannica (site) 97
Errors 30, 39, 48
Expedia (site) 95
Expertgardener (site) 98
Explorer bars
  Favorites 61
  History 73
  Media 42
  Search bar 69
  Third-party 116
Exporting
  Favorites 62

F

FAQ. *See* Frequently Asked Questions
Favorites
  Creating 58, 60
  Exporting 62
  Making available off-line 63
  Managing 59
Favorites bar 61
File extensions 46
Filtering messages. *See* Message Rules
Filtering software 134
Finding. *See* Searching
Flames 174
Flash player (add-on) 111
Football365 (site) 52, 91
Foreign and Commonwealth Office (site) 99
Forms 49
Formula1.com (site) 91
Frames 52, 55, 127
Free trials 12
Frequently Asked Questions 175
Full Screen mode 25

G

Golf.com (site) 91
Google (site) 79–80
Google toolbar (add-on) 116
GORP (site) 95

M

N

O

P